HEART, SASS & SOUL

Cover & Layout Design: Elina Diaz

For permission requests, please contact the publisher at:
Mango Publishing Group
2850 Douglas Road, 2nd Floor
Coral Gables, FL 33134 USA
info@mango.bz

For special orders, quantity sales, course adoptions and corporate sales, please email the publisher at sales@mango.bz. For trade and wholesale sales, please contact Ingram Publisher Services at customer.service@ingramcontent.com or +1.800.509.4887.

Heart, Sass & Soul: Journal Your Way to Inspiration and Happiness

Library of Congress Cataloging
ISBN: (print) 978-1-63353-974-7 (ebook) 978-1-63353-975-4
Library of Congress Control Number: 2019935683
BISAC category code: SEL045000 SELF-HELP / Journaling

Printed in the United States of America

HEART, SASS & SOUL

Journal Your Way to Inspiration and Happiness

GRETA SOLOMON

mango
PUBLISHING

CORAL GABLES

Praise for *Heart, Sass & Soul*

"*Heart, Sass & Soul* is an inspirational (and practical) guide to harnessing your creativity and using self-expression to create a better life."

—**Karen Swayne**, features and health editor, *Prima* magazine

"In a world where we are often bombarded with other people's stories, it is vital for our well-being and success in life to make contact with our own stories. *Heart, Sass & Soul* is the essential guide for how to create that meaningful relationship with self and then become the author and authority of your own story."

—**Zita Tulyahikayo**, systemic coach and hypnotherapist

"Behold! You are holding a bright pearl of love. A guide that bridges between your inner being and its outer expression. This work is coming from a mature and ripe place, with deep personal and professional experience. How blessed we are to be gifted with Greta's work which is profound and inspiring, yet light and accessible."

—**Yair Sagy**, yoga teacher, healer, and facilitator at Armonia Alpujarra Healing Retreat Centre

"A welcome and stylish exploration of writing as a way of uplifting your life. Sensitive, sassy and creative."

—**Malcolm Stern**, psychotherapist, author and co-founder of Alternatives

"Writing is a powerful tool in delving within, in learning who we are and what we need, and in building a beautiful life on our own terms. Greta Solomon's *Heart, Sass & Soul* is an invaluable, accessible, and practical resource that helps us do just that. It is filled with insightful, inspiring, and interesting stories and exercises. And it is no doubt a reference that you will return to throughout your life, throughout different seasons, transitions, and phases. Because it'll help you discover and rediscover who you are."

—**Margarita Tartakovsky**, writer and associate editor at PsychCentral.com

"Greta's wisdom and warmth shine through every page of this wonderful book. It's like being gently but purposefully guided toward a more accomplished version of yourself through writing and discovering your voice and your inner light—the you that you've always known you could be! This book has really helped me not to waver or stumble with my writing, but to stride confidently forward."

—**Anya Hayes**, Pilates teacher, MBCT mindfulness coach, and author of *The Supermum Myth*

"Keeping a journal has been a daily practice for me for many years. Journaling enriches my life as it helps to hone my craft as a writer. Writing down my thoughts clears my mind and helps me discover the topics that are really grabbing my attention. Greta Solomon's book is the go-to guide on the art of journaling."

—**Joan Gelfand**, author of *You Can Be a Winning Writer*

"Greta is to writing what Marie Kondo is to tidying. This is a marvel of a book which explores how you can find your creative voice and help clarify your thoughts through the lost art of writing. Creativity is, Greta says, the missing piece of the wellness puzzle, and in this book she shows you how to tap into your own creativity and use it to overcome issues and express yourself more clearly. Through it, we can rediscover the cathartic power of creative writing."

—**Georgina Fuller**, freelance journalist for national newspapers and magazines, including *The Telegraph*, *The Guardian*, and *Modern Woman*

"Greta Solomon reminds us of the value and importance of living a reflective, self-reflexive, and creative life, with enjoyable and gently challenging exercises, prompts, and wisdom, along with her own fresh and supportive voice."

—**Deborah Alma**, emergency poet (prescribing poems from her 1970s ambulance) and author of *The Emergency Poet: An Anti-Stress Poetry Anthology*

"We all know that journaling can be a powerful self-care practice; Greta artfully shows us HOW. This is an insightful, inspiring book empowering us all with the tools of self-expression. Very liberating!"

—**Suzy Reading**, chartered psychologist, mind editor at *Psychologies* magazine and author of *The Self-Care Revolution*

"As a writer, I know firsthand how therapeutic it can be to order your feelings on paper (or on a computer). This book is a wonderful resource for people who want to go deeper and really explore both positive and negative emotions."

—**Annie Ridout,** journalist and author of *The Freelance Mum*

Also by Greta Solomon

Just Write It! How to Develop Top-Class University Writing Skills (McGraw-Hill, 2013)

For Krister, Savannah Grace, and Leonie Joy.
With love, always.

TABLE OF CONTENTS

INTRODUCTION

When my mother was a young girl, she played the piano. And when her family moved, they took her beloved piano with them. But it wouldn't fit in the entrance to their new flat. They tried every which way to get that hunk of wood up the stairs, but it wouldn't budge. And in that moment, her piano playing life ended—it just didn't fit. Fast forward to around twenty years later and she was determined that her children would play the piano. Each of us duly went to lessons, but we never found the magic that she had experienced. That was her path, not ours, and we could never replicate the love and joy she felt for the music of the keys.

The path to self-love is difficult to navigate if it is littered with thwarted dreams and silenced music. It's no longer made-to-measure Valentino. Instead, it's more hand-me-down from an aunt two sizes too big, or from that whippet-thin cousin whose thigh is the size of your wrist. It doesn't fit. It tugs. It pulls. It itches. It scratches.

We can also pick at our wounds, compulsively, like the urge to pick, pick, at a scab until the freeing feeling of getting it off is replaced by the wincing rawness of unhealed skin. This is when we can become susceptible to criticism. Throwaway comments, insensitive observations, and downright nastiness can fester, and if there's no creative buffer, they can take hold. They can worm their way into your life, your psyche, your experience. Like a piece of wood made gnarled and moldy, it can seem as though your self-expression is tangled. The unwanted thoughts, fearful tries, and inevitable failures that are par for the course when expressing yourself can seem like clear signs that it's "game over."

(UN)SPOKEN AGENDAS

Let's look at criticism for a moment, because if you're anything like me, you'll have heard a lot of it in your life, from a variety of angles. Here is some of the criticism I have heard:

* You're too quiet and sensitive.

* You don't know how to get along with people.

* You laugh too loudly.

* You have short legs (yes, really!).

But what is interesting is that for almost every criticism I've heard from someone, I've heard the exact opposite from someone else. I say almost, because unfortunately, no one has ever told me I have long legs!

Here is some of the praise I've heard:

* You're one of the most outgoing people I've ever met.

* You've got such drive and determination.

* You're really good at building relationships with people.

So, who is right and who is wrong? And what does it all mean? Well, it means that words come with an agenda. People say things to get us to behave in a certain way. For instance, "You're too quiet" could really be someone saying, "I'm not comfortable with silence." And, "You laugh too loudly" could mean, "I feel depressed and your laughter reminds me of how unhappy I am." But instead of stating a flaw or weakness in themselves, others flip it back as a criticism— hoping that you'll mold yourself to suit them.

So ultimately, the only thing that matters is what we believe. The stories we tell ourselves and the world hold the key to our individual happiness. If you live by other people's agendas, then it's likely that you'll behave in ways that don't serve your highest self.

Can you relate to this? To the need to please, to be liked, to be loved? You might feel that need so much that you take the criticism, and, like a sculptor, you begin chiselling away at yourself until—over time—your structure falls. You took too much away here and left not enough there, and now you're broken and in pieces. So, you have to try and put yourself back together. Except now some pieces don't fit you anymore. You're new and different, and not necessarily better. You wish you had never started chipping away at yourself. But now you can't stop chasing some illusion of perfection that was never there and can never be there.

WHERE IS THE TRUTH?

When you embrace, believe, and embody criticism without questioning what's behind it, you can start to believe that you're not good enough. That's when your perception of the world becomes skewed.

A key sign is that you keep finding yourself in situations where criticism, bullying, and harsh words are commonplace. That's not necessarily to say that you are being bullied yourself, just that judgement, cattiness, and "calling people out" seems to happen all too frequently. Plus, if you're the one that people find fault with, you can start to feel less and less. Worse still, you may be left with no idea how to remedy the predicaments you find yourself in. And if there are no unfriendly people like this in your life, it doesn't mean you're off the hook. Maybe you have a critical inner voice, bullying you, pushing you around, and telling you you're not good enough.

Maybe you're telling yourself that you're a failed piano player who doesn't deserve to have music in her life. Maybe you're telling yourself that you're just not "good" at writing, you can't spell, and your grammar is crap. Maybe you're telling yourself that you want to write, you really do, but you don't want to dig too deep. What if your ex-boyfriend, grandmother, or childhood best friend sues you after reading the things you wrote about them?

That's not to say you need to believe you're the greatest, the best thing ever, and all superior. That's a fast track to an emotionally empty life. Instead there's a more optimal way—a middle path of love, one where you don't judge anything about yourself as good or bad and instead view it as information. Get to know yourself with an open heart and accept what you find. Then write what you find, express yourself, and take care of *your* needs first. Put fear to one side and create first.

Love and acceptance are gifts we desperately need to give ourselves. And they're essential for living a fully expressed life. In the coming pages, you'll find stories, ideas, food for thought, writing tools and techniques, and creative challenges and exercises that will help you to write your way to a self-expressed life. I'll coax you into expressing what you truly think and expressing what you truly feel. And I'll help you to write through the darkness until you pierce shadows of light.

I'll also look at the negative events that happen to us all, which are trying to guide us. The catch is that if you're not attuned to reading the signs and serendipities, the world will look bleak. But try to look a little deeper and a little closer. If you can squint your eyes and peer through the looking glass of life, you'll see that signs and serendipities abound. You'll see them dance across your eyes, pointing out the path to self-love.

WRITING CAN CLEAR A PATH TO SELF-LOVE

So, WHO am I? Well, I'm not a love expert. (Who is? I think each of us is a work in progress.) But I *am* a writer, teacher, and creative writing coach. I've also lived a rich and varied life, and I'd like to share what I've learned. And it's perhaps surprising that I want to do this, as I grew up wanting to hide. In fact, I think "easily embarrassed" is a phrase that accurately sums up my early childhood.

But over time I became adept at hiding in plain sight—on stages and in auditoriums. I sang, danced, ran, jumped, and played music. I was Deputy Head Girl in middle school and Head Girl in high school. One friend nicknamed me "shiny happy person" after the REM song. Yes, I smiled a lot, and I had a shiny forehead—something I thankfully seem to have grown out of. I smiled and mixed, and all the while I hid. I mean, I was outwardly positive and friendly. I got along. But inside I felt that no one really understood who I was.

So, I wrote—songs at first. It was 1988, and I would listen to Madonna songs on repeat on my tinny cassette player and write down all the lyrics. Then I would pick them apart to figure out the structure and why this rhymed with that, and so on.

I became a little nine-year-old connoisseur of love songs. I wrote and wrote about love and loss, love and loss—the two themes that define most adult lives. But I also started to realize that writing could be powerful, because it could help me to speak up for myself. So I started to put my thoughts on paper in other ways. I wrote letters to my favorite magazines, *Hi!* and *Look-In,* and got such a buzz when they were actually published.

Here's an example of one where I gushed about my favorite TV program: "I think the *Wide Awake Club* is brilliant. The bed-making competition is fantastic. I think the WAC team must be rich, because they give such a lot of prizes away." I mean, it was hardly Shakespeare, but it gave me a taste for the power of words.

Since those days, I've written and written and written: two nonfiction books (including this one); a novel (currently unfinished); thousands of articles (some published in magazines, some stuffed in drawers, some languishing on old hard drives); morning pages (three pages of stream of consciousness writing, first thing—as inspired by Julia Cameron); poems; more songs; blog posts; press releases, newsletters, speeches, award entries, and articles as a director at a business-to-business PR consultancy; journals; affirmations; shopping lists (both literal and spiritual); and scribbles here, there, and everywhere.

I continued to ask for things. For instance, after I graduated from university, I wrote letters to virtually every women's magazine in London, asking for a work experience placement. A couple took me up on my offer, and that's how I became a journalist.

I realized that through writing, I could ask for things that I wouldn't dare to speak out loud. Better still, I could write things into existence: things that were never there before, except for wishes or dreams in my head.

Writing unlocked so many doors for me (and not just because I became a journalist who got paid to interview celebrities, go to events, and drink champagne at parties). I think it was because I continued to write to people and ask for what I wanted. And when there were very dark, difficult times, writing was a helpful friend. In the year that I turned thirty-one, my mother committed suicide, and I wrote reams and reams about my feelings, which allowed healing goodness to flow. It was highly therapeutic, and those hours and hours of writing helped me to chart a new path.

A SAFE SPACE TO OPEN YOUR HEART

Writing allows you to be quiet enough to listen for the signs and serendipities that can guide you toward your highest self. Bad stuff will happen, and we desperately need a way to make sense of it. Writing can help you do that.

I'll never forget the words of Yair Sagy, an openhearted healer and teacher I met while taking part in a juice fast. He said, "Your heart has remained open because you're a writer, because you've been consistently writing throughout your life." Yes, I hid everywhere— except on the page. It was all there, written in ink, and it showed me the way time and time again.

I don't know if you're also the type to hide. But I'll bet that you're the type who wants a little bit more. But to get "more," you've got to go within. Writing is my way of doing it. For some, it's yoga or meditation, or painting or sculpting. For others, it's a weekly trip to a farmer's market and then back home to cook up a delight. Maybe for you it's a wonderful pick and mix of this and more.

For me, writing brings me back home. I love writing. I love words, their potential, and the goodness they can bring into life. They can heal, help, and harmonize. They can find a way when there is no way.

But what if you feel blocked and stifled? What if you write, but you never really say what you need to say?

Well, I've been there.

For my first six or seven years of being a journalist, I couldn't freely express myself when writing. There's a quote by "Red" Smith that I love. When asked about how he got his newspaper column done every week, he said, "You just sit at your typewriter until little drops of blood appear on your forehead." That's how it was for me too.

I was "good" at writing, but it came at a huge price for me. It simply wasn't easy. My block (or my writing personality) was governed by fear. (We'll look at this more in Chapter 1, and you'll figure out which kind of writing personality you have.) I used to leave all my writing until the last minute and only get it done through fear: fear of losing my job or of losing my colleagues' respect. There was so much strain and pressure that it was exhausting.

There was one time where my writing personality worked against me in a big way. My first journalism job was at a businesswomen's magazine. It was the kind of place where you worked for a year or two as a deputy editor straight out of journalism school before moving on. While looking for my next gig, I was invited by IPC Media (now part of Time Inc.) to interview for a position at a new women's lifestyle magazine that was launching. I was invited to a trial day, and all was going well until I was asked to write a sample feature. And I just couldn't do it. I kept crossing out and rewriting sentences. I couldn't decide on the angle, the introduction, or anything for that matter. In the end, I submitted a paragraph. Yes— just *one* paragraph. I will never forget the look on the editors' faces. I can laugh about it now, but at the time it was mortifying.

Ironically, my next job (which I got a few weeks later) was in the same building. I was hired as a features writer at another women's magazine, covering someone's maternity leave. I was twenty-three, and on paper it was the *dream job*. I should have been having the time of my life. But I didn't feel authentic, and I felt creatively blocked. I didn't have the easy flow of ideas that I have now. I didn't feel that I had a voice. And I felt like I was on a conveyor belt, churning out articles. I just didn't feel creative.

So when my contract was up, I went freelance as a journalist, cranking out articles for newspapers and magazines in my force-driven way. But crucially, I decided to explore my creativity and see where it led. I enrolled at a London drama school and starred in adverts and short films. I became a travel writer and explored health and wellness. I did voice and improvisation classes. I wrote lots of songs and poems and got some of them published.

All of these experiences helped with my self-expression. But things really shifted for me four years later when I began studying lyric writing at Berklee College of Music.

The first thing we learned was a technique called object writing, which is something that songwriters use to help them get raw material for songs. And it was life-changing. I will introduce you to this technique later in this book and show you how you can put it into practice in your everyday life. What's for sure is that object writing opened me up and I was finally able to write freely and expressively. And this way of writing crossed over into my journalism work and all the other writing work I did after that.

After undergoing such a transformation, I realized that I wanted to train as a life coach and teacher and teach people to write. I started off tutoring students. I taught them object writing and other self-expression and writing techniques I'd learned while earning my lyric writing diploma. And it was a big hit. I got a reputation for turning C students into A students *because* they became self-expressed writers. And I turned my methods into the book *Just Write It! How to Develop Top-Class University Writing Skills.* I found what I was supposed to do and realized that I loved helping people to better express themselves in writing. And that's what I have been doing ever since.

The crucial thing is that I feel completely free and able to express myself in writing both privately and publicly. In your own room and own space, you ought to be able to write freely. Cry. Laugh. Feel the feelings. And sometimes you need to write something that is raw and not for public consumption, something that wouldn't please your eighth-grade grammar teacher or your boss, but that pleases you.

But if you do want to shape your writing into a finished piece, then that's great, and I'm going to share some tools and techniques that will help you do that. In fact, creative self-expression is cyclical, and if you can add technique to heart and soul, you can keep going deeper down through the layers. I'll also share my tips for going a step further and creating personal, creative blog posts. Plus, if you're already an accomplished writer, the stories and lessons in this book will help you go deeper and inspire you to access your writing space from a position of love.

I'm committed to doing all I can to help you to better express yourself in writing and live a full, rich, creative life. As such, my vision for *Heart, Sass & Soul* is about more than the words you'll read in this book.

HERE ARE THREE WAYS THAT YOU CAN GO EVEN DEEPER IN YOUR SELF-EXPRESSION

1. Stay in the Loop via Social Media and Connect with Other Readers

Expressing, connecting, and sharing go hand in hand. If you feel called to do so, please share your insights on social media while you read. Tag me @greta.solomon on Instagram and @greta_solomon on Twitter. Use #HeartSassSoul so that other readers can find you.

2. Sign Up for Journey Beyond Journaling

This is a free, five-day writing challenge designed for people who yearn to write more. If you feel your voice has been suppressed in some way—this is the challenge for you. Visit www.gretasolomon.com/challenge to receive daily videos and creative exercises that you can complete in ten to fifteen minutes. These will support you in releasing mindset blocks, getting in your body, awakening your senses, and opening your heart. You'll kick-start your writing and creativity and begin to see what's possible for you—beyond the pages of your journal.

3. Go Deeper with My Online Program in Writing for Creative Self-Expression

This is a completely tried-and-true, seven-week course in mindset, creativity, and craft. Using videos, audio recordings, and worksheets, I guide you to break through the blocks that hold you back. Through writing workouts, coaching questions, tasks, challenges, and tutorials, you'll wake up to your writing potential. Plus, you'll learn practical tools and techniques for writing articles and blog posts. By immersing yourself in this material, you'll begin to uncover your voice and learn how to use it. Find out more about this unique, life-changing program here: www.gretasolomon.com/online-course.

As my course participant, Janet said, "When I was young, I loved to write stories and wrote constantly as a way to express the angst of my teenage years. Unfortunately, this led to shaming, because those very personal journal entries were read by someone who used them to ridicule and criticize me. You are the first person to name and identify the damage done by this kind of shaming. After working through your course, I am recognizing that I am well on the way to healing that tender, violated part of my inner world. There has been a remarkable, gradual fading of the critical inner voice. Now, I have a structure to work within and techniques to practice, and it has given me a sense of direction and purpose."

This is my desire for you too—direction, purpose, and the safety of having practical tools and techniques to guide you on your journey.

Most of all, I want you to know that what you hold in your hands now, or consume via your screen or audio device, is an invitation. It's an invitation to begin to live a fully expressed life.

A LOVE LESSON, AS TOLD TO ME BY YAIR SAGY

Finally, I'd like to end this introduction with a short meditation. Put your hands on your heart and imagine the space within. Feel your heart and then see your inner child. Look in her eyes and give her a hug. Love her. Take care of her needs. Be kind to her. Protect her from harm. Listen to her. Laugh with her. Give her treats. Take her for a day out. Be a parent to the little girl inside you, and remember this—when you love yourself, it's easy to put up boundaries because you don't fear rejection. You can easily say "no." Repeat the affirmation: "I love myself." Repeat it again. Then imagine the roar of a lion and its power and say, "I am creative, fertile, serene, and powerful like a mountain."

Be love. Exude love. Let it fill your whole body and radiate outwards. And remember that writing for creative self-expression will help to set you free.

PART 1

ANSWERING THE CALL

CHAPTER 1

CLEARING THE BLOCKS TO SELF-EXPRESSION

When you write, do you feel truly able to express yourself? Are you able to *really* say what you need and want to say? I always ask these questions at the beginning of my workshops in writing for creative self-expression.

When writers are struggling with the world, they often put their angst into words. For instance, the 1950s beat poet Allen Ginsberg poured all his suffering into *Howl*—an epic poem about his dissatisfaction with life. His publisher was then put on trial for printing obscene language. Yet to Ginsberg, those words simply expressed what he thought and felt, nothing more; nothing less. His world contained gay sex, and he didn't hide that. He freely expressed himself.

You may be thinking, well, time has moved on—now anything goes. But we are all taught in our daily lives to censor ourselves, and we're socialized to do this from a very young age. This censorship not only extends to our social relationships, but even to our private thoughts, and, for some of us, into almost every waking moment of life. Rather than face a "trial," we figure it's easier to just write (or say) something bland, something every palette can handle. But if you do this enough, it becomes a habit that's hard to break.

So when I ask that question, "Are you truly able to express yourself?" it's no surprise that 90 percent of people say, "no."

FOR MOST PEOPLE, WRITING COMES WITH A LOT OF BAGGAGE

Writing is free. It costs just a pen, a piece of paper—and perhaps a coffee (maybe a bulletproof one for extra brain power). But for many of us, it's a minefield. On the surface of it, the blank page is non-judgmental. All it asks is to be filled with marks. It's completely impartial. It doesn't mind whether the marks are scribbled or perfect looking, or if they're grammatically correct. But when we bring ourselves to the page, we bring a lifetime of baggage—some of it accumulated from around the age of five, the first time we ever put pen to paper.

Now, of course, there are some people for whom writing freely is a weapon. I'm thinking of people who practice hate speech; the alt-right; the bitchy columnists who spread racist and sexist propaganda; and the internet trolls who delight in taking people down. However, I'm sure you'll agree that these folks are not truly self-expressed. Their bullying behavior is a mask for something else, and though they may write freely, it's not with joy and love. I hope those people find health and happiness. But they're outside the scope of what this book is about. And I don't want to waste another word on them. You who are reading this book—yes, *you*! You are the one I have written this for.

HAVE YOU EVER BEEN GRAMMAR-SHAMED?

By this, I mean when you've written something heartfelt or creative, and the response you get back is all about your grammar or punctuation. This type of *mostly unhelpful* feedback is commonplace. People who don't know how to write or who are excellent technical writers with blocked self-expression can *only* focus on the mechanics of writing. They miss the nuances and ignore the feelings and the messages behind the writing. And, if you listen to them, you'll get on a fast track to being blocked yourself, like my client who can remember vividly the specific nun who shamed her as a child, whose voice she still hears when she's writing. Another client used to write professionally but then was deeply shamed by a senior editor who resented her naivete and enthusiasm. She remembers the specific occasion where she was lambasted in front of her work colleagues and how it shredded her self-confidence.

The solution is to practice the exercises in this book and just let them unfold a path for you. Clients have told me that my work has helped to take away the shame they felt from being dyslexic and that they used to be self-conscious about their writing, but, after practicing for a while, the self-consciousness just disappeared. Others have healed from the wounds left from parents or partners reading their innermost thoughts and picking them apart.

They were finally able to let the joy of creative self-expression take over. And that's the thing. We don't want to get too serious and bogged down, nor try to drown out the negative voices or hurl insults back. We want to listen. So ask yourself, "When, where, and why have people shamed you into thinking your creativity is bad?"

Chapter 1: Clearing the Blocks to Self-Expression

This is something that we explore deeply in my online program. We need to accept the answers and make a space in our hearts for joy to bubble up. Then we use that to express ourselves—our true selves.

THE COMMUNICATION PYRAMID

The communication pyramid is a handy tool to help you to visualize the different layers of self-expression that you can access.

At the top, we have the mind—the place where most of us write from. I don't teach this at all, not even when teaching in the business and academic worlds. When you write from the mind, the writing is dull, formulaic, and rule-based. It cannot inspire or move anyone to do anything—least of all yourself.

Second down, we have the body. This layer is useful and is the zone of the practical writing techniques that you may have learned in a how-to course, or while reading a how-to article on the internet. I also teach these in many of my writing workshops and online programs. The heart and soul are, of course, the focus of this book. We'll do lots of work around these, and there'll be lots of stories and examples to keep you on track.

Finally, at the bottom, there is voice—the much-discussed holy grail for writers. Every writer wants to find their voice. But you can't really find it. As you go down the layers of the communication pyramid, you uncover it. It's the sum total of the mind, body, heart, and soul. Because although I said I don't teach the mind stuff, of course it comes into play. The mind figures out how to organize the dance of words, phrases, and sentences. My method is to ensure you get out of its way. Give it lots of time and space, and the heart and soul will speak to it for you.

The communication pyramid

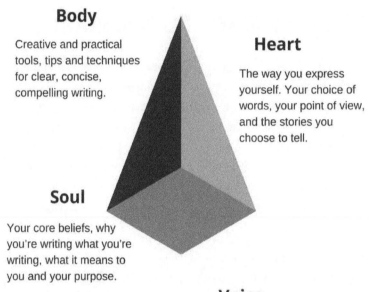

Mind

Grammar, sentence structure, writing hacks, and rules and regulations.

Body

Creative and practical tools, tips and techniques for clear, concise, compelling writing.

Heart

The way you express yourself. Your choice of words, your point of view, and the stories you choose to tell.

Soul

Your core beliefs, why you're writing what you're writing, what it means to you and your purpose.

Voice

Your distinct personality and style – an authentic version of you. Everything should feel resolutely YOU.

Grab a Notebook and Answer the Following Questions:

* Which place do you write from most?

* How can you access the deeper places? Brainstorm some solutions that you think might work for you.

Don't wait for the perfect time to write. If you have an idea, pull out your phone and jot it down. Put all those sentences together and you may have a full piece! Learn to love first drafts, and don't be shamed by spelling mistakes or grammar errors. When it comes to creative self-expression, they're simply not in the job description. Walk, run, shower, wash up, go for a drive. Do things that switch off your mind and see what bubbles up. Then write it down.

FACING UP TO WHAT LIES BENEATH

Quieting your mind and getting honest with yourself is tough. In the early 2000s, I spent a few years exploring acting as a possible career and signed up for an acting course at Pineapple dance studios in London's Covent Garden. The first session was fun, until the teacher told us our homework. The task was to bring in a picture of yourself as a baby and talk about your childhood. I felt I couldn't do it—that it was too personal. And I walked around with a knot in my stomach all week, dreading having to reveal myself publicly.

But I did it, and it felt good to face my fear. And it wasn't even as though I shared anything earth-shattering, just some run-of-the-mill family stuff. After the second session, we were given another assignment. This time we had to choose a significant event in our lives. Then we would have to communicate it the following week to the others in the class, using only our eyes and faces. Now I was really scared. I had never done anything like that before. Where inside me could I find the means to express that? I told myself that it wasn't really acting and that it didn't make any sense. What about the words? Why couldn't we just *say* how we felt? The following week, I found a reason not to make it to class. And the following, and the following...until the ten-week course was over, and I'd spent a couple of hundred pounds (that I couldn't afford) on only two group acting classes!

When I *did* enroll in full-time drama school the following year, my voice teacher cautioned me, "You have to find your own voice. Everything you do is about championing the voices of others." And it was true. I was, and at heart am, a journalist. I love doing interviews and telling people's stories. I love packaging advice in fun, fresh ways. I love digesting information and retelling it. But at that time, I was simply unable to go deeper in my communication. In any case, after a couple of years, I realized acting wasn't for me and continued on my path as a writer.

If *you're* having trouble accessing the lower layers of the communication pyramid, the collection of beliefs and behaviors that make up your writing personality are probably getting in the way.

We all have a writing personality that protects us from going too deep, that prevents us from accessing that place inside and drawing it out. It's self-protection. But it'll get in the way unless you bring it to light. Figuring out your writing personality and how to navigate it can allow you to reap dividends. In doing so, you shine a light on your behavior when you have a pen and paper in your hand or you're at the keyboard.

WRITING PERSONALITY TYPES

Note: these descriptions relate to the public writing you do, which is probably at work. But we take these public personas home with us too, and our writing personality seeps through every time we write.

Perfectionist Petra

Your attitude is that your writing is either perfect or worthless. You spend ages on one piece and feel that nothing you do is ever quite good enough. Ironically, your work has plenty of errors because you always want your writing to be exact and precise. You're highly conscientious and a hard worker.

Fretful Fiona

You hate seeing your boss's, editor's, or colleague's red marks on your work. So you play it safe and don't take many writing risks. This means you tend to follow set patterns in your work and don't like to try out new techniques or ideas.

Could Do Better Betty

You simply never put 100 percent into anything. You know that you have huge potential but instead prefer to do just enough to get by. Occasionally you pull out all the stops and write something magnificent. But then you go back to your "easy" life—which of course doesn't feel easy on the inside.

Fun-Seeking Femi

You prefer not to think too much and would much rather be active and outdoors that cooped up with a notepad and pen or hunched over a computer. Having fun is the most important thing, and writing just doesn't compete with other activities. But secretly you yearn to write.

Slapdash Susannah

You whittle work off at an amazing speed, but your writing is littered with silly errors that would have been spotted with a little more care and attention. You also leap in and start writing without formulating any kind of plan.

Last-minute Lorraine

If you have a deadline, you often miss it, or make it just in the nick of time. This is simply because you don't give yourself enough time to write. With every piece of writing you do, it's as though you're competing in a hundred-meter race because you avoid it until the last minute.

One-trick Olivia

You quite like writing certain things: your blog or Instagram posts, for instance. But when it comes to something you find challenging, you freeze up. Sometimes, you can get going but find it hard to finish. You wonder if you really have the skills to write properly.

Grab Your Notebook and Answer the Following Questions:

* What's your writing personality (in your own words)?

* Which of the writing personality types did you identify with?

* How do they sabotage your writing?

* What strategies could you put in place to stop them taking over?

Now consider this:

✳ How can you get your writing personality to work for you, not against you?

FEAR—that's the word to remember. All these writing personality types are governed by fear. Shaking things up helps you to bypass this fear. Quite simply, you forget you're scared, you lose the coping behaviors, and writing just happens. So don't be afraid to shake things up. In fact, page by page, that is what I will urge you to do in this book. The following quote by the philosopher Nietzsche has become my mantra over the years: "One must still have chaos in oneself to be able to give birth to a dancing star." We just need to remember that there is safety in the storm. When you ride the wave, the raging tide cannot harm you. When you yield to its force, you are strong. It's only when you try to resist it that the chaos can turn into destruction.

A great way to get past the fear is to move. So, the final exercise in this chapter is a moving one. Your challenge is to pull on a pair of comfy shoes, go for a solo walk, and shake off the fears.

THE MAGIC OF MOVEMENT (AKA WHY YOU NEED TO WRITE ON THE GO)

Walking and thinking and writing go hand in hand. Getting into your stride and mapping out where you want to go on the street allows your mind to do the same with your thoughts and ideas.

Ferris Jahr explained this perfectly in an article called "Why Walking Helps Us Think" (published in *The New Yorker*). He wrote, "Since the time of the peripatetic Greek philosophers, writers have discovered a deep, intuitive connection between walking, thinking, and writing. 'How vain it is to sit down to write when you have not stood up to live!' Henry David Thoreau penned in his journal. 'Methinks that the moment my legs begin to move, my thoughts begin to flow.' " I couldn't agree more. And no, I didn't just include that quote for the snigger factor of the word "methinks." Although I dare you to go around using that for a day, just for fun!

But I guess that's the point. Movement is fun, and walking shakes things up, helping to clear the cobwebs to creativity. It pumps blood and oxygen to all the muscles in your body.

In fact, for the past few years, I've been blogging on the go, pounding the pavements, and typing my posts into my phone. It struck me that when I get out into the world, armed with a little inspiration, the ideas (and my writing) just flow. I realized that if I consciously sit down and think about what I want to write, the writing often comes from my head, and not from my heart. In contrast, my writing is far more heart-centered when I put myself into an alpha state, where my subconscious can flow.

In my first book *Just Write It!* I wrote a little about this alpha state:

> *Ideas are like radio waves that float all around us waiting for us to tune into them. And when you alternate intense thinking with periods of rest, you often find that you open your antennae for flashes of inspiration. This usually happens when you're doing routine activities such as walking, running, washing up, or taking a shower. These types of activities increase alpha brainwaves. These put you in a relaxed enough state for your intuition to kick in, or for you to have an "aha" moment.*

The trouble is that in our society, we do too much pushing and not enough allowing. Many of us take quotes such as Thomas Edison's "Success is 99 percent perspiration and 1 percent inspiration" to heart. And that can mean that we end up chaining ourselves to our desks.

The following exercise is about giving yourself permission to move, to roam, and to explore—to shake out of your skin and move into the magic of your imagination.

Writing on the Go: The Instructions

Walk for thirty minutes while thinking, daydreaming, looking, and seeing. Make sure you have a notebook and pen with you, or a smartphone where you can write down whatever comes into your head.

Before: Set an intention for what you want to write, or think about an issue or topic that you'd like to ruminate on. Alternatively, you can think about what's bothering you today—those (good or bad) thoughts you just can't shake.

During: Well, there are no real rules. Just do anything that gets you walking and into a good rhythm. You could go to the park, or go window shopping, or explore a part of town you've never been to before. Once ideas pop into your head, stop and write them down as fast as you can, and then continue walking.

After: Once you're back from your walk, reread what you've written, and, if you feel inspired, use your favorite bits in a finished piece of "work." By work, I mean a Facebook or Instagram post, a little note that you put on your fridge door, or a verse you decide to save on your phone. If you like what you have written, honor it by saving it somewhere special.

I love this exercise, because it allows creativity to percolate and brew. When I run retreats, we do this together. We begin in a pack—talking and laughing—before wandering off our separate ways to walk our way to writing. I recommend doing this walking and writing exercise regularly (as often as you can). If nothing happens the first time, try again. Wait patiently for creativity to happen, and trust that it will. If nothing more, you'll have gone for a head-clearing walk.

YOURS TOO, CAN BE THE TRUEST VOICE

If your energy is flagging, I hope this story will perk you up. You may have heard it before—it's the story of Florence Foster Jenkins, which was made into a film of the same name in 2016. If you haven't seen it, I recommend that you get yourself to a movie download site, pronto! The film is a heartwarming display of passion. Florence is a woman who has had syphilis for fifty years. She's always known she could die at any moment, so she always felt she had nothing to lose by following her passions. She had wanted to be a concert pianist but couldn't due to problems with her hands. So, she ran a successful music club with her boyfriend for more than two decades.

Then, in her twilight years, she decided that she wanted to sing. The trouble was she didn't have a "good" voice. It was either flat or completely out of tune. Plus, she had poor phrasing and terrible breathing. But she sang with such gusto and passion, and with so much of her heart and soul, that despite her concert audiences laughing at her, they also fell in love with her.

Toward the end of the film, she reads a terrible review of her performance in *The New York Times*. She looks to her boyfriend for reassurance: "I was never laughing at you. Yours is the truest voice I have ever heard," he says. But the shock of the review sends her health into a downward spiral. And finally, on her deathbed, she says, "People may say I couldn't sing, but they can never say I didn't sing."

Make sure they can never say that you didn't write.

Don't allow anguish, fear, and blocked creativity to stagnate. Get moving and get writing. There is true magic in movement. You just have to put one foot in front of the other.

CHAPTER 2

FORGING A NEW CREATIVE IDENTITY

In 2003, I went to see a destiny reader. Yes, that was her official job title! I had met her a year earlier while researching and writing a feature called "Married for Seven Years But Are We Compatible?" The idea was to use lots of different tests to see if on paper and anecdotally, a happily married couple were actually suited to one another. A Feng Shui expert whom I'd worked with on several other features recommended her. And she was amazing! She used Indian astrology, which is very different from the Chinese method. By simply taking their dates and times of birth, she used her scientific system to pretty much tell them everything about their past, present, and future. She was so spookily accurate, that a year later I found myself in her kitchen, eating delicious homemade curry while she talked me through my own destiny.

As we talked, she told me things she couldn't possibly have known. Then she told me my future lay in writing and speaking. I guffawed. Writing—YES. Back then I was a journalist, and writing was a big part of my life. But speaking—I told her NO WAY. Ahem, I am now a professional speaker, and leading workshops, talks, and retreats is a huge part of my life. But back then, it seemed unbelievable. And it just goes to show that we often don't know what future we're stepping into.

> **Her main point, however, was that I needed to
> stop forcing and pushing at life.**

She went on to explain that life is made up of time periods (for me, it was ages 0–9, 9–29, 30–34, 35–54, and I forget the rest). In these periods, only certain things can be achieved, she explained. It doesn't matter how much you want something or how hard you try. You can only achieve the success, the lessons, the blessings, and the fortune that these time periods are able to bestow on you. It was the first time I had heard about the concept of divine timing. That key things in life unfold when *they* are ready to unfold—not when we want them to.

When you view your own life through this lens, there is no one set-in-stone schedule for when you should complete society's milestones. Instead, if you learn the lessons and work through the thoughts, beliefs, and behaviors of that period—then you can move into the next cycle *without* your old baggage. And in that new cycle, new things are possible. The aim is to use creativity to navigate the space between the time periods, when an old way is dying and a new one hasn't yet begun—and to remember that we're all on different schedules.

HARNESSING YOUR INNER POWER

In the early days of my career, money was short, and my freelance writing lifestyle meant that I didn't always know when my next paycheck was coming. So I read the classic Napoleon Hill self-help book, *Think and Grow Rich*. I didn't grow rich (in money), but I did learn a thing or two about inner power. Hill introduced the idea of sex transmutation—something I still find fascinating. Sex transmutation is when you turn the energy of sexual desire into creative fuel and use that to drive ahead and forge a new path. It's when you turn on your emotions and feel positively charged. For our purposes, it's about falling in love with writing and creativity.

In her book *Big Magic: Creative Living Beyond Fear*, Elizabeth Gilbert asks her readers to imagine that their creativity is like a hot relationship they're in. If it was, they would steal time for it, stay up all night to be with it, and think about it all day. Fusing your life with that kind of desire and intensity is extremely powerful.

To achieve this kind of desire, you need to get firmly into your physical body first (layer two of the communication pyramid from Chapter 1). Whether consciously or not, we're taught from a young age to be out of tune with ourselves. We sit at desks for most of our school days and are told to think and solve intellectual puzzles. If we later work in an office-based job, we're told to do the same, with a few workouts thrown in before or after work, or perhaps at lunchtime. Moving and being firmly IN our bodies is often discouraged. And yet, this is where much of our power is.

Love her or loathe her, I think Madonna in her heyday (from the *Get into the Groove* days until *American Life*) was a mistress at stoking sexual energy and using it to create. Watch any of her videos and you'll see that her energy is firmly grounded in her body. Remember that energy is simply a force that we can use for good or bad. And misplaced energy that's not properly harnessed can turn into fear and anxiety. This can then become depression and lethargy, which can keep us stuck. Like wading through syrup, it can feel burdensome and heavy—even if we consciously know that the sweet stuff is there for the taking, if only we can transform and transmute it.

To harness your energy, you simply need to do things that make you feel good in your body. Notice that the word I used was "feel," not "look." How do you feel after a bubble bath, after spritzing on your favorite fragrance, after listening to your favorite music, after eating your favorite food, or after watching a really great show? Don't deny yourself the small things that make you *feel* good in your body. Make a list, if necessary, and check them off as you integrate them into your life. Notice what things, people, and situations foster positive energy.

According to Napoleon Hill, once you're in this state of heightened intensity, you become "turned on" by what you're thinking about or working on, are more expressive, and feel more driven to take action. But crucially, this desire doesn't come from the mind, but instead comes from the body. This puts you in a state where you can be expressive, driven, and able to surrender to the flow of life—all at once.

There is a potent, fertile power in this. So although Hill called this sex transmutation, it has nothing to do with whether you're having sex or not. You could be celibate while still stoking your sexual energy and using that to power your life.

Forging a new creative identity is about harnessing your energy so that you can surrender to the flow of life and go with the tide, instead of pushing against it.

I believe we ought to surrender to life. Surrender to the process. Surrender to the journey. And when a shift is ready to happen, it'll happen. And then *everything* will change. It will be a new life and a new way of living. That doesn't mean we have to enjoy everything or condone what is going on. *No.* Instead, we need to do everything in our power to rally with life, to fight what needs fighting, and to develop, change, grow, and learn the lessons. And then we need to trust and let go.

Of course, this is easier said than done! So, if you're thinking "*What? How the hell do I do that?*" I *feel* you. I felt that way too, for a long time, and I didn't understand how not to push, how not to set goals and use my logic and try and forge a path through sheer guts and determination. But the answer was hidden in the final two pieces of advice that the destiny reader gave me. She told me that I needed to write a diary and I needed to talk to God. At the time, these two things seemed so simple, I almost overlooked them completely.

But writing was (and is) a path to getting into the flow of life and not pushing against it. And talking to God (in whatever concept I saw or could see God) was just about connecting with divine energy and the forces of life outside of my limited self.

This is pretty much what all the great self-help teachers have ever taught. But it's not enough to understand it logically. It only makes a difference when you can understand it in your bones.

Exercise: Six Not-So-Simple Questions

Grab a notebook and answer the following questions:

1. Are you pushing at life and trying too hard to control what happens?

2. If so, how could you surrender and go with the flow instead of pushing? (Note: this doesn't mean that you stop pursuing your dreams, just that you try a different way.)

3. Are you frustrated that you're doing or have done the right things but feel flat or listless? What are the unwanted side effects of feeling this way?

4. How are you getting in your own way in going for the things you want?

5. Is there something you really want to do, but you never find the time or energy to actually do it? What would life look like if you had space for this creative pursuit? (I'm assuming it's creative, OR that you can do it with a creative spirit!)

6. Do you want to write but rarely find the time and energy to do so? What does the energy of being a writer look like to you?

Finding time to create, or to do *any* creative activities, can feel daunting. The act of writing, or singing, or drawing, or painting, or making *anything* can feel like a huge mountain to climb. This can be especially so if we're painfully disappointed by our efforts when we do "pull our finger out" and create. But here's the thing. It's possible to transmute sexual desire into an emotional desire for life, writing, and creativity. So, it's also possible to transmute fear into fuel. It's OK to be scared, because fear isn't the enemy—stagnation and being stuck are. The remedy is to keep getting firmly in your body. So keep physically moving, and use the exercises in this book to reset your mindset and give you emotional and creative fuel.

I believe in forging a creative identity where you're constantly composting and nurturing ideas, and where writing isn't just the act of using a pen or tapping away at a keyboard. Instead, it's a lifestyle that starts with a daily nurturance of your own emotional, creative (and sexual) energy. If you feel an impulse to sing in the shower—do it! If you feel an impulse to shake your hips to music on the radio—do it! If you feel an impulse to pull a funny face to make your friend laugh—do it! If your shoulders are stiff and you need a massage—give yourself one! Flex your toes, arch your back, feel how good your body can feel when you notice its sensations. It's vital to nurture your fertile, creative power so that when you *do* write, it's a true expression of *who you are*. When you look at it this way, the subtitle of this book, *Journal Your Way to Inspiration and Happiness*, is a powerful call to action.

Looking at writing in this way can also help to take away the guilt if you feel that you *should* be writing but aren't. Instead of being the act of putting pen to paper or tapping away at the keyboard—writing is a lifestyle. And the things you do to *prime* your writing are all part of the process.

EXPLORING YOUR CORE BELIEFS

The rest of this chapter provides tools and techniques so that you can go deeper down the communication pyramid (outlined in Chapter 1) to the soul level, which is layer four. This layer is concerned with your core beliefs, why you're writing what you're writing, what it means to you and your purpose. My aim is that you, my dear reader, will see yourself—your creative self—in a new light, which will make the practice of writing a lot easier. It's vital to trust that spirit, insight, and inspiration will come if you get yourself into the right emotional state. Remember to actively work on "turning yourself on" and then allowing goodness to flow. Turn procrastination on its head and actively use time to your advantage. There's no hurry. So, slow down and savor the journey.

Exercise: Understanding People, Power, and Control

1. Once, when an interviewer asked the actress Helen Mirren if she had any regrets in her life she said, "I wish I had told more people to f*ck off." Hear, hear—me too! Helen felt that she had spent too much time playing the "good girl." Where do you regret playing the good girl in your life? What effect has this had?

2. How does this "good girl" energy trickle down into your writing? What are you afraid to write about and why?

3. Has anyone ever betrayed your writing trust (by reading your diary for instance)? Even if they haven't, does writing feel like a safe space for you? If not, why not? **Note:** We'll look at tools and techniques for not judging your writing later in this book, but it's great to create this awareness now.

4. Where does fear sneak in and trip you up? How can you transmute your fear into fuel?

Exercise: Getting to the Heart of Your "Why"

The questions below will help you figure out your vision and values and get to the heart of why you want to write. If you have a strong enough "why," it can help you to bypass whatever fears you may have and help you get to the deeper layers of self-expression. We all live from our values, and if we don't know our "why," we can be driven by the wrong things.

1. Why are you drawn to writing? What do you write about (or want to write about)? Why?

2. What are you passionate about? Why?

3. What truly brings you joy? Why?

4. What do you most want to share with your writing? Why is this so important?

5. What benefits do *you* receive from putting your thoughts and feelings in writing? Think in terms of the emotional, spiritual, and social benefits. Why are these so important?

If you get stuck, think of spiritual benefits as the intangible things that make life good. For instance, after a good night's sleep, it's likely that you'll experience more harmony both within yourself and with your environment. That's the spiritual benefit. The emotional benefit could be that you feel good, and the social benefit could be your smoother interactions with others.

Take time with these questions (as much time as you can). They look deceptively simple on the surface, but if you take time to truly dive into them, it's likely you'll unearth some gems.

Is Your Writing Personal or Public?

If you're not yet sure whether you want to create a body of work to share or just want to write for your own personal health and well-being—this exercise may help.

Get yourself in a cozy, comfortable place and close your eyes. Now imagine that it's your book launch. Or picture that your tell-all article or blog series has been published, and you've shared your heartfelt words with the world. Imagine people talking about your innermost thoughts and feelings and all the things you have shared. How do you feel? Scared? Empowered? Recognized? Seen? Validated?

There is no right or wrong answer to this. Some things are meant to be shared immediately. Other things need to ripen before they're shared. Other things ought to always be private and kept within the pages of your journal. It's certainly not necessary to reveal other people's secrets nor air people's laundry. But there can be immense power in sharing *your* view, *your* experience, and what happened to *you*.

As you continue to read this book and mine your personal headspace for the gems it contains, what you want to write about and why ought to become clearer and clearer.

Why Breath Is Flow (and How to Keep the Flow)

Finally, with all this talk of fear and fuel, and transmutation, and telling more people to f*ck off—don't forget to breathe!

Breath is incredibly powerful because it carries a quantifiable bioelectric charge. Western medicine calls this the negative ion (while in the East it's called chi). Think of this chi energy as being able to nourish the body in a similar way to food and water. Studies have shown that deep breathing increases the number of negative ions in the body and helps to detoxify and recharge our cells. Deep breathing also aids digestion, eliminates stress, encourages deep sleep, and stimulates brain function.

Breathing can create these changes because it's directly linked to our emotions. The downside of this link is that when we feel angry or afraid, we often subconsciously hold our breath. If we do this often enough, we hold onto tension and rob the body of its natural energy. The major problem is that most people don't even realize they're doing this, because breathing is an unconscious activity. So take a deep breath. In fact, take several really big ones, deep from the center of your belly and your being. Connect with the energy you need to go and forge your new creative identity.

CHAPTER 3

TAPPING THE CREATIVE CURRENT

So how can you consistently tap into the creative current and let it run wild and free? We've seen how paying close attention to what you do before, during, and after you write matters. Writing isn't about sitting at a grand desk with a quill pen, composing your magnus opus. Keep remembering to move, walk, breathe, and sweat. Keep getting firmly into your body so that you can tap into the core of your creative self.

The exciting news is that this chapter is all about the actual creative writing—and, for this chapter, you'll remain firmly in the heart space (layer three) of the communication pyramid. I'll introduce you to the technique of object writing. It's a method that some songwriters use to get soulful song lyrics, and it can completely transform your writing. It helps you to break through blocks and fears so that you can write freely and easily.

When I run workshops and online programs, I always ask the participants why they've come and what they want to get out of the workshop or program. The answers ALWAYS involve blocks or fears. Here are some of the responses I've heard:

* "I write case studies for work, but I always leave them to the last minute. I'm afraid that if I really put a lot of effort in and get negative feedback, then it will mean I'm not a good writer.

I don't want to face up to that. So I don't really put myself into the work, and I just write in a really dull way."

* "I work in communications for a management consultancy. I write articles and do a lot of ghostwriting for people in the company. I feel that my own voice is becoming lost. I'm trying to write a novel and want to start a blog. But I haven't got a clue about what I would blog about.

* "I work as an architect and think and write in a very technical way. I yearn to be more creative."

* "I'm a professional photographer, but I want to be better with words so I can write compelling Instagram captions."

* "I've dreamt of starting a blog for years, but I'm terrified of getting started and of sharing my work."

* "I feel that I've been drained of the joy of writing over the years. I work in law and have become so used to writing in a left-brained, logical way. I've been made to feel that anything else is unacceptable."

* "Most of my career has revolved around writing, but mostly other people's writing—editing and translating their work so they can get published. I finally want to prioritize *my* work."

* "I have been writing professionally for about ten years, mostly journalism, plus two nonfiction books. I would love to explore a more creative way of writing. This is something I have wanted for a long time but simply haven't allowed myself the time to do."

* "When it comes to my writing, I feel like a washed-up actor, as though my best work behind me."

* "I've spent so much time and energy raising my kids that I need to do something for myself. I want to be the writer I know I can be—before it's too late."

* "I work in academia, and, for me, my creative writing is a secret. I need to come out of the closet."

**Do you recognize any of these responses in yourself?
Why are you reading this book?
And what do you really want to get out of it?**

Knowing what you want and your intentions before you start writing is super powerful. It helps you to anchor your writing, because you're clear on exactly which blocks or behavior patterns you want to break through.

For all my clients, writing is such an intricate part of their lives. Most have a longing to make their writing more formal. They feel a need to put a stake in the ground and accept that their thoughts and feelings deserve to be put in writing. Yet their fears and negative emotions are getting in the way. There's a push-pull between wanting to share and being scared to share.

Now, it's time to put an end to that.

BEGIN BY CREATING YOUR JOY LIST

A joy list is a list of objects that spark joy in you. The idea is to curate this list and then use it to tap into your self-expression. You'll use your objects to master the tool of object writing. This is where you take an object and write about it using all of your senses. These senses are seeing, hearing, touching, tasting, feeling, and moving. Object writing is a powerful tool by itself. But by using your joy list, you get a double workout. You practice your writing skills *and* harness your joy.

My Challenge to You: Spend Five Days Writing for Joy

Why five days? Because five days *feels* joyful. It's long enough to feel like a daily practice and short enough to commit to—even amidst our daily pressures and strains. Especially so, in fact. When there are too many demands on your time, your needs, wants, likes, and desires can be ignored. Your inner voice can diminish daily, little by little. That's why you need to write. It's a quiet protest, a quiet power.

Of course, there's a lot more you can do after five days. You can dive deep into metaphors and literary techniques and a host of other writing strategies. And in Chapter 7, I'll introduce you to a tool for making metaphors. But five days will allow you to begin to feel a flow. It will get life and breath moving in your words again.

How to Create Your Joy List

Now, this is simple—so don't overthink it. Simply go through your house or flat and collect the objects that spark joy within you. Start by choosing just five. Don't simply choose ones that are fashionable, or expensive, or desirable to others. Choose the ones that mean something to you, even if they're rusty, old, and in need of some love. You'll give them that through your object writing. This "spark joy" process has been made popular by Marie Kondo, the famous face of the Japanese art of tidying up. You don't have to tidy up, you just need to feel and trust your instincts.

To help inspire you, here is one of my joy lists (meaning that the list you create doesn't have to be *the* definitive one).

1. **Wedding picture:** My husband and I walking through the woods in Addis Ababa reminds me of the utter freedom we felt when we eloped. We started off our marriage *our* way!

2. **Hard copy of the December 2017 issue of British *Vogue*:** This was the first issue edited by Edward Enninful. I waited in line for two hours outside the *Vogue* offices in London to get my limited edition copy and meet the man himself.

3. **"Woody" piggy bank:** A little piece of my childhood via *Natwest Bank*, circa 1988. The bank gave a piggy bank to every child who opened an account, and, with each twenty-five pounds you put in (up to a maximum of one hundred pounds), you got another member of the pig family!

4. **Miranda perfume from Fragonard, the French perfumery:** In 2005, I spent several days in a small village just outside Cannes while attending Midem (the music industry version of the Cannes Film Festival). On a day trip to Grasse, I went to the amazing Fragonard perfumery. And I have been wearing their heady Miranda scent ever since.

5. **Our turquoise sofa:** In my first studio flat, my landlord told me to buy whatever furniture I liked and he would reimburse me. So I chose a gaudy turquoise sofa from Ikea that I absolutely loved. After moving to more grown-up apartments and houses, I chose more grown-up (read: boring) furniture. But I finally went back to my roots and picked out a vintage style turquoise sofa for our latest London home.

For each object above, I've given an explanation of why I love it and why it brings me joy. This is just to give you some context. You don't need to do this—your love and joy will come out in your object writing. Later in this chapter, I'll give you an example of a ten-minute object writing session I did focusing on the Miranda perfume bottle.

If you feel called to do more, you can create a joy list altar in your home—and take a picture of it. You can use this as a positive reminder when you're at work or out and about that this week, you are focusing on joy, and you are writing for joy! I'd love to see your altars, so feel free to share them on Instagram. Tag me @greta. solomon and use the hashtag #HeartSassSoul

So, What Exactly Is Object Writing?

Object writing was invented by Pat Pattison (a professor at Berklee College of Music) to help songwriters get raw material for their songs. It's likely that some of your favorite songwriters and recording artists rocked up to the studio one day and followed the steps that I'll outline below. But this technique isn't just for songwriters—it can completely transform anyone's writing skills.

OBJECT WRITING CAN...

* Get you started (it kicks your writing muscles into gear)

* Bring your writing to life

* Increase your powers of description

* Improve your ability to give quick stories, examples, and analogies

* Build your confidence to tackle more difficult pieces of writing

It's easy to master, fun, and gives fast results. When we do it in my workshops, people often want more. They want to reexperience the freedom they felt while writing from the heart—not the mind. Object writing is all about accessing the heart (layer three of the pyramid), and it helps you to produce heart-centered writing. The questions in the latter half of Chapter 2 were all about the soul (layer four). You need both, along with other tools and techniques, in order to uncover your writing voice, which is the fifth and deepest layer of the communication pyramid.

HOW TO DO IT

Take an object from your joy list and write about it—with a pen and a piece of paper—using only your seven senses. Look at the object and focus on what you see, hear, touch, taste, and smell, the movement of the object, and how you feel about it. You do this in a short burst of either ten minutes, five minutes, or ninety seconds. Having a limited amount of time makes you laser-focused and stops your mind from jabbering and getting in the way.

It helps to think more about the seven senses before you get started. I'm sure you're all familiar with the first five senses, but it can take a little extra practice to describe objects in terms of feeling and movement.

Think about feeling as being more than your emotions. For example, does an object (or your associations with it) make your heart beat faster or cause your muscles to tense up? When it comes to movement, don't just think of the obvious movement an object makes. Instead, also think about your internal movement when interacting with an object. Think about the strange sensation you feel when getting back on solid land after a boat trip. Is your body moving in response to the object?

OBJECT WRITING IN SEVEN STEPS

1. Write the following headings at the top of the page to remind you of the senses you need to focus on:

   See Hear Touch Taste Smell Feel Move

2. Set a stopwatch for ten minutes, five minutes, or ninety seconds.

3. Spontaneously write down whatever comes to mind about the object. Write with excitement and interest. Be as specific as possible with your descriptions and images.

4. You don't need to stay completely focused on the object, so don't worry if random words and sentences tumble out. Just go wherever your seven senses lead you.

5. Write in full sentences if you can, but don't worry if it's easier not to.

6. Keep your hand moving across the page, and don't stop to cross out words or correct spelling mistakes.

7. Only amend spellings, grammar errors, or other mistakes when you've finished. Yep, this is hard. But resist the temptation to stop and judge. Keep your flow, and don't worry if what you write looks clunky or disorganized.

EXAMPLE

Here's an example of a ten-minute object writing session on a bottle of perfume (Miranda by Fragonard).

Disclaimer: I wrote this freehand while in Starbucks one evening but did a few minor edits while typing it up (to make it publication ready!)

Cool, silver, stainless steel containing such rich warmth and beauty. Burnt oak, sandalwood, and cedar with the heady smell of freedom and summer days. The glug of champagne and flowers and life—a life on the precipice of earth, and air, and water, and rain. I hear the beat of bees, of rivers flowing and pulsing. So warm and inviting, enveloping me in a chocolate kiss. Beaconing to me like freshly baked cookies, warm with promise and crumbly with pleasure. And the stink, stink, stink of heady summer bliss.

The bottle feels cool and fresh to the touch. The juxtaposition of cold with the delicious drops inside. Each one like a bubble of soap that contains the whole rainbow in one drop. Knowing that I can be a different person when I step into this scent. One who eats croissants, no, not eats but nibbles them between delicate blood-red lips. And drinks red wine and coffee in the cafés of Paris, and cuddles by the fire in winter. While the noses are at work in the factory churning out scents of such pure delight.

The taste of vanilla, not ordinary, not normal, but rich and succulent on the tongue. I feel warm and bright, and earthy. I feel like I can plant my feet firmly on the ground and spin my mind to new dimensions like a kaleidoscope, or a maze in a secret garden. Like the key to the door of another world.

The bottle is a burgeoning promise, of a summer on the edge of reason when I didn't know what to feel or think. When I had been betrayed.

Seeing the golden liquid slosh in a container that doesn't belie its beauty, I see that truth and beauty isn't always on show. That tin of temptation makes me feel alive whenever I spray it. I am intoxicated and drunk with delight. I feel enlivened and bold as I carry around a secret. Like going to the cinema in the afternoon and seeing a film just for me. Like taking a bubble bath and spritzing on perfume just for me. For my ears and eyes only. I feel untouchable and touchable all at once and endorsed by love, and by happiness. By me and Fragonard and the secrets of my scent.

I've taken the tool of object writing into the corporate world and have taught it as part of writing skills workshops. On one particular occasion, I shared it with the management team of a technical company who had hired me to help them write more creatively. Object writing isn't supposed to be grammatically correct or technically perfect. It's supposed to unlock creativity. Everyone was having great fun with it. But one of the communications professionals was disgusted by it all. She went very red in the face as she spat out that she couldn't take me seriously as there were so many copy errors in the object writing sample I'd presented to the group. I checked and there were some rogue errors that had slipped in. But her outburst was a sign of just how creatively blocked she was.

If you or others are outraged by errant commas or apostrophes, it's not the grammar that's the problem. There are underlying self-expression issues there. So remember to always think back to the communication pyramid in Chapter 1. Which layers are you and others operating from, and why? And remember that people use grammar as a weapon to shut others down by ridiculing their mistakes instead of listening to their message.

SOME THINGS TO REMEMBER AS YOU WRITE

* Think of your object writing as an outlet for your creativity. Don't try to write; just turn on the tap and let the words flow out.

* What you write doesn't have to be "good." Write with love and joy, and don't think about validation. Don't think at all— just keep your pen moving. Tell yourself that what you're writing is good enough and keep going.

* Don't write for any specific audience, just express yourself in a fun, fresh, lively way.

* Circle or underline your favorite words and phrases afterwards. It's easy to judge yourself harshly while you're

writing, but, if you go back and actively choose your favorite bits, it's likely that you've spontaneously used metaphors, similes, and rich, lively language. The idea is for you to see that, when you open the floodgates, you can naturally write in a creative way. Here are my favorite words and phrases from my piece of object writing.

◊ A life on the precipice of earth, and air, and water, and rain (notice the repetition of the word "and")

◊ I hear the beat of bees (notice the alliteration of the *b* sound)

◊ Enveloping me in a chocolate kiss (such a beautiful image)

◊ The delicious drops inside (notice the alliteration of the *d* sound)

◊ A bubble of soap that contains the whole rainbow (beautiful image)

◊ I can be a different person when I step into this scent (notice the sibilance, i.e., the repeated *s* sound in step and scent)

◊ Summer on the edge of reason (I've inadvertently used the title of Helen Fielding's second Bridget Jones novel)

◊ Tin of temptation (notice the alliteration with two *t* sounds)

◊ The secrets of my scent (finally, there's more sibilance here)

Exercise: Your Daily Joy List Practice

Pick an object from your joy list: any will do, as you will write about a different object each day.

Set an intention: Your object will have meaning to you: what do you intend to feel, do, be, or have through writing about this object? For example, if you're writing about a picture of you and your kids, maybe you want to reconnect with the positivity you all felt in the picture. If you're writing about a painting that lights you up, maybe you intend to use the energy of that to make your own art.

Write the headings in your journal: Go to a fresh sheet and write, "See, hear, touch, taste, smell, move, feel."

Use a stopwatch: Set it for either ten minutes, five minutes, or ninety seconds. I recommend you do ten minutes on your first two days to get you in the swing of things. Then after this, you can mix it up. Do what feels good to you (and what you have time for). And use a stopwatch instead of a regular watch so that you're not distracted by keeping time.

Write: Keep your hand moving across the page and don't stop to correct any errors.

Reflect: How did you feel? What did you learn? What will you do differently next time?

Circle your favorite words, phrases, and images: This ought to be fun, and it's likely that you'll be surprised at the cool images you come up with—my clients usually are! Plus, the beauty of object writing is that it helps to develop your voice. The words you use will become unique to you. Through this process, you start to express yourself in a way that is resolutely *you*, because only you can sense the world the way you do. You might spontaneously produce fun titles, ideas for new projects, snippets of a blog post, or a poem. Look at what you've written as raw material and save it somewhere special. You may want to use it later.

Share if you feel called to do so: Email a trusted friend, share in a private Facebook group, or post some snippets on social media using the hashtag #HeartSassSoul. Feel free to edit what you've written. It's only the initial object writing process that needs to be free-flowing.

Repeat this process for five days in a row: Take a different object each day, set an intention, set the clock, and go. And if you feel inspired, do it for longer than five days—picking a new object each day. When I first discovered this technique, I did it every single day for a year. There are no limits.

And that's it! Congratulations on completing five days of writing for joy.

Object writing is a workout—the more you do it, the stronger your writing muscles become. You'll find metaphors and powerful images tumbling out. You'll spontaneously write in a rich, heartfelt way. Why? Because this ability is already within you. Writing from the heart is about remembering and relearning the gifts many of us threw away as children—especially if we were ushered into sensible careers or left-brained pursuits like science and engineering. But joy is energy, and it can spark positive action. And it can help to bypass this type of social conditioning.

When you purposefully move into joy and creativity, you begin to expand into your highest self—the self that is grateful, loving, and kind. Object writing isn't a magic wand, but it can open the floodgates to help take you where you want and need to go.

Chapter 3: Tapping the Creative Current

CHAPTER 4

EMBRACING MOMENTS OF MAGIC

For me, magic is a change in perspective that allows goodness to flow into your life. It's about tapping into something outside yourself and experiencing the flow of good fortune. Do you have a fortunate friend? I'm thinking of my old school friend Noreen (not her real name). She always saw opportunities. She smiled at life. There was an ease about her—a sense of inner confidence and well-being. Her inner beauty shone through, which made her glow. And in return, luck found her.

To embrace moments of magic, we need to create an environment in which to nurture these qualities. If you increase your willingness to embrace serendipity and the goodness it brings, you'll begin to view life differently. You'll see that detours and roadblocks are simply a part of the master plan.

I started writing this book in 2016—at least, that's what I thought. But a funny thing happened while I was backing up my computer. Being the old-school gal that I am, I back up everything on an external hard drive. My usual one was full, so I rummaged around in my desk drawer and found a hard drive that I hadn't used since August 2011. I took a nosy through the files and found a book proposal I had written. It was called *Write Your Own Life* and was about writing for creative self-expression. It was rough around the edges, but there was a proposal with detailed content for each chapter and an introduction, plus reams and reams of research taken from academic journals. It was the *exact* same idea as the book you have in your hands—expressed in a different way. The crazy thing is, I had completely forgotten that the proposal even existed.

This shows me that dreams find their way back. And things that need to be written hang around until they get written. So don't worry if you feel you have turned your writing dreams aside one time too many. Follow the lessons in this book; read the stories; live and love; and your dreams will come back.

So, how are you getting on with your object writing? Did you do it for five days? Don't worry if you didn't. This book is as much about planting seeds and following breadcrumbs as it is about writing. All the exercises and challenges are suggestions, not writing prescriptions. Granted, there are exercises and tasks to complete. But you don't have to get up an hour early or commit to producing a page a day, or even a page a week. It's about slowly and surely developing a life you love that allows you to find the time, the momentum, and the ease to write for creative self-expression. There is a quiet, beautiful power in that. So above all, aim to arm yourself with knowledge and tools so that when the time is right for you, you can spring into action.

Having said that, if you have created your joy list and done your object writing, then it's a big high five from me!

THE SIREN CALL OF SERENDIPITY

So, let's get back to the magic with a little discussion about serendipity (also sometimes called synchronicity). The word "serendipity" was first coined in 1754 by Horace Walpole, who defined it as a "fortunate happenstance" or a "pleasant surprise."

Dictionary.com defines it as "an aptitude for making desirable discoveries by accident." As mentioned before, it comes from a shift in perspective, showing up in the world a little differently, and being open to magic and miracles. Not water-into-wine type miracles, but the small coincidences that can change the course of your life—the unexpected meetings, the chance encounters, and the grateful knowing that you are in the right place at the right time.

So, what has serendipity got to do with journaling your way to inspiration and happiness? Well, everything. Positive optimism is *so* powerful. In the space between being single and meeting my husband, I read a book called *Meeting Your Half-Orange: An Utterly Upbeat Guide to Using Dating Optimism to Find Your Perfect Match* by Amy Spencer. It contained a lot of writing exercises all aimed at getting you feeling happy and joyful, clear on what you want, and trusting that the right love will come to you at the right time.

We never know exactly what combination of thoughts and actions produce a result, as life is such a tapestry. But I met my now-husband a few weeks after reading the book. I recommended it to a friend who also met her husband. There's a lot to be said for serendipity. In fact, I wouldn't have met my husband at all had a volcano in Iceland not erupted that weekend. He was due to fly out to Ethiopia that day to see the results of the charity he worked for. But his flight was canceled and the trip postponed, so he decided to hit the town instead and ended up in the same nightclub as me.

He was younger than me, visiting from Norway, and was only due to stay in London for a few more months. So, nothing made logical sense. But we made a dinner date anyway, and just clicked! We got engaged later that year. We got married the next year and had a daughter the year after that.

My point is that sometimes opportunities, even the very right ones for us, don't come dressed up in the packaging we expect. Positive optimism is about taking chances, doing things you wouldn't normally do, stepping out a little into the zone of discomfort, and deciding to live a life less ordinary. That's when you're able to enter the zone where magic happens.

MY FIRST MAGIC-MAKING TOOL IS THE LIST

So often I hear people say that they don't know what they want. They want to start a business, but don't know which business to start. They want a relationship, but feel stuck in a pattern they can't break, and, besides, they have no idea what qualities their perfect match would really have. They've never *really* given themselves the chance to sit down and quietly tap into what they really want. Does this sound familiar? Whenever you're in a situation you don't want to be in, write a list of what you DO want.

Exercise: Take Yourself Off to a Café (or a Quiet Corner of Your Home) and Write a List of What You Do Want

Choose one area of your life, and really go for it. To supercharge this exercise, you can write your list in the present tense using the words "I have / I am / I do," as though you already have what you desire. Aim to be uncensored, because it's not about what you think you can get but what you want, what your heart desires. It's about what truly brings you joy. Refer back to the "why" exercise in Chapter 2 if you get stuck, and make a list based on one of your answers. Then take a small action, whatever it may be—as long as it is something that brings you closer to something you want.

Exercise: Keeping a Magic / Serendipity Journal

You know when you buy a new car, a coat, or a stroller for your child and then suddenly see it EVERYWHERE? Well, it was always there, you just weren't primed to notice it. You had no skin in the game and so had no reason to notice it. Well, it's the same with magic. You don't notice it until you already have a bit of it. So at first, you'll need to train yourself to look for it. This is where your magic / serendipity journal comes in.

Whenever your day allows you a little downtime, jot down the little coincidences, moments of serendipity, and pieces of good fortune that have happened. Aim to do this for a least a week, and review at the end of the week. What good stuff has happened that you would normally overlook?

Don't discount anything. You may have received a freebie at the train station on the way to work. A chance conversation at a café may have given you the piece of information you needed in order to move something forward. You may have nabbed the last shirt in your size at the summer sale. Anything and everything that brings a little rush of positive energy ought to be included. You can never have too much good stuff. Nurture it, and soon it will open the channel for more and more goodness to flow.

LISTEN TO WHAT YOUR MIND AND BODY ARE TELLING YOU

So with all this talk of magic and movement and possibility, now is the time to set the record straight that I am by no means a

Pollyanna. I know that there's a lot of bad sh*t in the world, and this isn't about discounting that. It's also not about discounting your negative emotions. They are there for a reason. They are a sign, and they are trying to tell you something, just like the moments of serendipity are positive signs telling you to "lean in" and ask for more. The negative emotions and events are negative signs telling you seek out less of whatever is causing them. So whatever negative signs and signals you are getting—pay attention to them. They're there to help you navigate your life. Perhaps you need to surrender, grieve, find work you love, find your voice, or really and truly love yourself.

Take the attitude that nothing is coincidental. If you keep hearing the same things from people—listen. If you keep experiencing the same old results (the ones you don't want)—listen. Consider these signs to be an invitation to try something new.

Likewise, if the only time you feel relaxed and happy is the brief period between Friday evening and Sunday morning, and then, as Sunday goes on, you feel dread welling up in your stomach until you're pricking with tears by the evening—consider it a sign that something needs to change in your Monday to Friday.

Our bodies and minds are ALWAYS giving us feedback. But if we don't listen to it, we can lose the ability to effectively interpret the signs and signals. Instead, everything feels like a massive ball of anxiety. Write your way through this, and use your journal to unpick what's really going on. This can be a long and messy process, so don't consider this a quick fix.

For instance, when I first started regularly journaling in my early twenties, I wrote a song called "The Wilderness Years," because that's exactly what it felt like—like I was in the wilderness. And those first few years were all about unpacking the past, and lots of hurt and pain that had long been buried. However, a lot of it focused on my frustration of feeling stuck. I needed to leave home, but I didn't have enough money to rent in London. I also didn't want to get a full-time job, as I wanted to work as a freelance writer and live a creative life. It was only when I did something completely out of left field, which was to get regular work as a tequila girl in London's bars and clubs, that I got the cash and confidence to change my life! I only worked as a tequila girl for six months, but that time was transformative.

However, it took about four years of journaling, expressing myself on paper, and trying out things in the world for this *real* shift to happen. And it took about another two to three years to get even more clear. But that's the thing, eventually clarity emerges, especially if at the same time you do things to physically move the energy around in your body. (Remember the walking task in Chapter 1?)

If you're in this messy or stuck stage, stream of consciousness journaling can come in very handy. Write down your thoughts haphazardly with no prompts, just write and listen for what comes up. After a while, you'll see yourself writing about the same things again and again. Consider this a sign—a sign to take action. If you're not sure which action to take, just do something—anything. Get the ball rolling, and change course once you're in motion.

Also, if you're in a stuck stage with your journaling and writing, take heart. When you see writers, bloggers, and social media influencers writing and posting prolifically, it can feel like you're the only one stuck in the same thought patterns. It can feel as if what you journal and write about is stuck and stale. But everyone goes through stages when their life (and their writing life) just doesn't flow. The tools in this book are designed to help with that, so use them as much as you can.

Finally, remember that you're not supposed to feel bad most of the time. We can't feel happy and joyous every moment of the day. But a fully expressed life is about getting to the heart of what you're feeling and why, so that you can keep resetting your emotional thermostat to joy.

GO WHERE YOU'RE WELCOME

While you're spending time getting in touch with yourself, make sure that your environments and the people in them are as supportive as possible.

After my fortieth birthday, I kept thinking that I ought to make a list of all the things I've learned throughout the years. But as I packed up the last of my party decorations, logged into my blog, and planted my feet firmly back on the ground—I realized that there is really only *one* lesson. And that is: *go where you're welcome.*

It applies to everything. To friends. Relationships. Jobs. Restaurants. Bars. Even the place where you get your morning coffee.

There are certain people and places who will welcome you with open arms and who will love you, who will get your sense of humor; who will appreciate your dress sense, your cackling laugh, and your very essence.

And then there are those who will turn their noses up at you—either literally or metaphorically—those who refuse to acknowledge you, and those who snigger behind your back and gossip about you as soon as you leave the room. And there are those who intentionally try to harm and hurt you. And life becomes sad and small if you spend time trying to get those people to accept you.

It really is a choice, and one that you can make with joy. So go where you're welcome, and go there with love.

So, as we close the first section of this book, remember that the greatest form of communication is the one you have with yourself. Remember to pay attention, follow the signs, surrender to the signals, and allow serendipity to work its magic. Focus on giving love time and space to breathe and grow, both in terms of what you love and who you love.

This love can then overflow into every area of your life, from work, to relationships, to your personal and emotional well-being. Of course, I can't make you any promises. But I hope, sincerely hope, that looking at your life under the microscope and seeking understanding will enrich you, enliven you, and awaken you.

PART 2

HOT SAUCE FOR THE SOUL

CHAPTER 5

CREATING LOVE FROM LOSS AND GRIEF

This second part of *Heart, Sass & Soul* is about remaining in the lower layers of the communication pyramid (as outlined in Chapter 1) and writing with heart and soul. This section is about your choice of words, your point of view, and the stories you tell. And it's about how these marry up with your core beliefs.

Part one of this book was all about shaking off the blocks; moving; exploring the magic of possibility; and experiencing the joy of writing freely and easily. Now, it's time to dip your toes into a deeper transformation—by mining loss and grief for the gems they contain. Some losses, such as bereavement, demand instant attention. Others are inconspicuous until they pile up on top of one another and suddenly suffocate. I've experienced both—from the suicide of my mother to the small, insipid losses that can come from not being self-expressed.

My mother was sixty when she died and, according to the coroner, was unusually healthy for a woman her age. Her suicide was a deliberate act, and it marked the beginning and end of so much. In the next chapter, I'll look at ways to make meaning from such dark times as this. But for now, I will focus more on what I call "everyday losses" (which, of course, doesn't diminish their impact in any way).

When I moved to Oslo from London in 2011, I moved for love—to be with my Norwegian husband. But I didn't imagine what pulling myself out of my home would actually feel like. I'm very independent and love traveling. But I'm also a highly sensitive person who is shy at times, and I'd spent most of my life in North West London.

While abroad, I continued to water and nurture the major relationships in my life. But I missed the small relationships, the tapestry of daily interactions. Plus, I missed the ease I had felt at slotting into life in London—a place so diverse, you can always feel at home.

Unless they're taken away, it's easy to underestimate the power of our small daily interactions, like the newsagent who knows your name and expects to see you on a Friday when you pick up a bottle of wine and the friendly next-door-neighbor who you can have an easy chat with. Yes, you can recreate these, and resew new connections. But the tapestry will forever look different. And sometimes, you just won't fit your environment.

If your daily interactions are less than optimal, you may not even realize just how much they affect you, your self-esteem, and how you view your life. If you're the only _____ [insert appropriate noun] in the village, then I'll bet you feel constricted in some way.

Looks and possessions, freedom and mobility, comfort and security, work and status: these are all things we can take for granted unless they are taken away. Who hasn't yearned to step back into the body of their youth—full of life and vigor? Or only missed the job they happily left once they no longer had their high-vibe colleagues in their life? Or found that leaving a relationship that didn't fit has left them out of sorts and afraid for the future?

It's not how big or small a loss looks to outside eyes; it's about how it makes you feel and how you deal with it. Because to be honest, no loss ever feels small. And big leaps and radical changes— even positive ones—can bring about a complex set of emotional responses that need to be unravelled.

Unfortunately, in our modern society, we have no socially defined ways of dealing with loss. We don't wear a black ring or armband to let others know that we're sensitive and need to withdraw. There's no socially accepted period of going within and coming out on the other side. And for the most part, life doesn't stop. Besides, for many losses, that would feel like pomp and circumstance. I've heard people speak of how "lucky" they are, how they ought to be "grateful," and how they feel guilty for admitting that the emotions of loss have reared their heads.

That's why we need to create our own tools. Because when the little losses add up, you can become tangled in a quagmire of depression that strips you of the energy you need to process those losses.

Traditionally, when the Japanese break objects, they mend them with precious metals. So a broken china vase would be fused together with gold. The gold symbolizes that the object is even more precious now that it's mended. I think this also plays out in life. Truly healed people are precious, because they're able to experience deep joy and can share their wisdom with others.

Connecting to the well of your being by letting your words flow can connect with the healing flow of love. Here are three tenets to help this process.

* Take time to grieve (including grieving your creative losses). A rejected screenplay, super-harsh feedback from someone you admire, or a stalled creative career all need to be

honored for the emotions they bring. Honor your losses, and don't diminish their importance.

* It's OK to be sad, angry, afraid, or upset, even if you're the one who has instigated the change. All losses produce emotions. Shedding old skin is painful—even when you're stepping into a bigger and better future.

* Let loss lead you to love. Create radical self-compassion by continuing to check in with yourself and writing out your emotions. Honor your journey and how far you've come.

THE BLANK SLATE

I'm now back living in London, but, in 2015, I was four years into my expat period in Norway. It was a usual winter, full of deep snow. I had a heavy cold and the lethargy that comes with freezing days and nights, diminished light, and pervasive gray.

The month before, my intuition had kicked back in after being dormant for a while. It led to me making some key changes in my daughter's diet—which to this day have made a massive difference. Living in a foreign country had shifted my inner compass, and the noise of my life had been louder than my intuition. But suddenly, there was calm. The snow was so heavy, and being under the weather, I almost didn't go. But my husband offered to drive me to Nesodden—the island just outside of Oslo—where the Create Your Vision Board workshop I'd registered for was taking place.

Now, vision boards were nothing new for me, but, amidst all the transitions involved in getting married, moving countries, and having a baby, it had been at least four years since I had created one. While taking that space and time to be cocooned in not only vision boarding but yoga and stretching, accompanied by miso soup and hot tea—I felt myself emerge once more. It was as though I'd gone underground as a means of self-preservation. But here I was once more.

I had never felt that I fit into my surroundings (in the cities and towns of Norway), but I began to realize that didn't matter, that I could create myself once again without fear of whether or not I'd be accepted.

And as it turned out, that inner shift shook off the cobwebs of loneliness and laid the foundations for connecting with people who were a lot more like me. I had found it hard to find fellow expats who were willing to have frank conversations. But finally, I did find local friends who were willing to communicate openly and honestly, who were kind and funny and friendly. And I reconnected with those who had been like that the whole time but who I hadn't really seen. And do you know what? That didn't come until I "got real" with myself. It didn't happen until I had said no to living with a low-level buzz of dissatisfaction.

I needed to wake up, and wake up I did. After years of focusing on teaching business writing, I started doing personal writing again and stripped myself of the image I'd thought I had to present. I enrolled in a now-defunct course called Blogging from the Heart run by the amazing Susannah Conway, and harnessed the true power of writing from the heart and soul. I started to *really* feel again, and I wrote myself into a new identity that took ALL of me into account. Before too long, I felt I had written myself back to life.

Navigating the Spaces Within and Between

When loss hits us, we enter "the great unknown." And at some point or another, we all face this. How we face it shapes our lives in so many ways. The space between jobs, friends, relationships, homes—anything, in fact—is fraught. There's no solid ground, because in that space nothing is certain. There are no rules, and life is unpredictable.

I wish I knew in the past what I know now: the best thing to do in that space is *nothing*—well, nothing aside from walking, writing, thinking, and going about your daily routine! Transition time is not the time to make major life changes or big decisions, because you don't yet know the lay of the land. If you make big changes from this space, you shake up the snow globe of life. This can plunge you into deep confusion while you wait for the snowflakes to settle.

You also don't owe anyone an explanation for your downtime while you're in transition. You're not a robot; you're a human being. If people can't understand that it's unhealthy to be productive and motivated 24/7—then wish them well in their bewilderment and continue walking your personal path. Don't feel pressured into publicly voicing feelings that you're still unraveling privately in your journal. This extends to social media. Despite what some experts may say, you are under no obligation to share anything (at all!) Plus, it can be far more authentic to write nothing when you're in chaos and confusion or are simply unsure. Only share when *you* are ready to share. And choose carefully who you share your innermost thoughts with.

Sadly, there are some unpleasant people out there who will encourage you to share so that they have ammunition to hurt you with later. They want you to share so they know where your weak spots are. That way, they can exploit you when you're off guard. Sociopaths and narcissists come dressed in the nicest clothing, and they don't always make their presence known. That's why, in the midst of loss and grief, you need self-love more than ever. You need to hone your inner wisdom and your inner voice. You need a strong sense of what is true and what is not. So never be afraid to bide your time, and to make your journal your first port of call before you venture outwards.

Exercise: Mapping Out the Pathway to Love

Here are some questions to answer. If you feel some aren't relevant to you, give them a go anyway. The answers may surprise you.

1. How do I feel?
2. Why am I feeling this way?
3. Who, or what, is triggering this?
4. Does how I feel change in different environments? What's the difference?
5. Is there an unhealthy environment I need to leave?
6. Is there a toxic person I need to reduce contact with or not see at all?
7. Who or what is getting in the way of me seeing myself as I really am?
8. What am I truly afraid of if I strip off the layers?
9. Who is never (or rarely) happy for my success, but seems to enjoy it when things don't go well?
10. Who doesn't think it's my birthright to be treated with love and respect?
11. Who do I suspect sniggers behind my back when I leave the room?
12. Who isn't open to my energy or doesn't appreciate my gifts? This can be either physical gifts and presents or the gifts you have to offer the world.
13. Do I feel unworthy of love?
14. Am I afraid to shine?

15. What do I need to finally accept about myself?

Take your time with these questions, and don't be afraid to seek out support in processing the answers. That's why counselors, therapists, psychologists, and soul sisters and brothers exist: to help us along the way.

Exercise: Creating Your Loss List

So, what have you lost that you feel is significant enough to put in writing? Remember, you don't have to share this with anyone, but it can be about anything from a former friend you used to have raucous nights out with, to a gorgeous scarf you left on the train. It could be the body you had before you gave birth to a child. It could be a childhood pet, or the loss of a person—someone deeply significant. For example, I still find it difficult to reconcile the fact that I donated my beautiful blue guitar to a charity shop before moving to Oslo. It was a highly practical decision—I mean, I didn't actually play the thing! But I had been with my mum when I bought it at The Ideal Home Show, and it seemed like a little piece of her.

Create a loss list of some big and small things you feel you need to process. In the same way that you compiled your joy list in Chapter 3, you could go around your house or flat—this time sensing what's missing. Or you can do a mind-map or brainstorm lots of losses, then hone in on five, at least initially, that you want to work with.

My invitation to you is to do object writing on these things— whether they are objects or not. In this way, you are able both to honor them and to uncover thoughts, feelings, and ideas that you perhaps hadn't realized that you had associated with these losses.

The aim of this exercise is to view these losses through the lens of creativity and in turn begin to transmute them so that you can heal.

And remember, no loss is too small to be healed from. Small things can make a massive difference to how turbulent life feels.

Exercise: Write a Love Letter to the Person, Thing, Place, or Feeling You've Lost

Finally, I love this exercise for its simplicity and power. What do you want to say to the person, thing, place, or feeling you've lost? Put it in writing. Make it an occasion. Use proper notepaper, and sit down at a desk to write. And then release it. Scrunch it up, safely burn it, or tear it into a million little pieces. And then do it again, if necessary.

When it comes to loss and grief, eventually clarity comes out of chaos. But first you have to bathe yourself in the intention of love. When we've lost something out there, the only way back is to find what's missing inside. And writing is invaluable for doing this.

CHAPTER 6

MAKING MEANING IN DARK TIMES

This chapter is an invitation to break through darkness into light—by making meaning. This can be any darkness (including a dark night of the soul). But I think the most bleak darkness of all is the death of a loved one, even if that loved one died through miscarriage.

As with the everyday losses I discussed in Chapter 5, it's essential to honor the transition and put self-care at the forefront. There are organizations on hand that offer free professional support. But remember that they won't beat a path to your door. You have to seek them out. And make sure you follow your instincts in your bereavement and grief journey.

This is something I didn't manage to do too well. Instead, I was swayed by opinions, conflict, and drama. I was wracked with fear and woke up to regular night sweats. I was vulnerable and easily manipulated. I didn't recover my inner strength and firm footing until at least two years after my mother's death. And overriding it all was the feeling that there was no safety net for me.

I tried desperately to make meaning, and I don't know if I did. But what I did do was write. And I'm here to tell you that, as a creative person, I feel that all you can do with the dark times in your life is to attempt to make meaning out of them, to try to create something out of the pain, sadness, and longing, to try find a chink of light and follow it where it leads.

So, in this chapter, I don't really have answers—*you* hold all the answers, deep inside. But I do have questions, suggestions, and virtual hugs. Similarly, I don't have a road map. But I can hold your hand as you navigate your unknown. And one day, as the old parable says, you may see that you were *not* buried, you were planted.

LET'S START WITH TWO LESSONS IN LOVE

1: Nothing Is for Free

I believe everything in life creates some kind of energy exchange. So, you always pay for everything—even if you don't hand over a penny. It's so important to be mindful of the interactions you have with others. Too many of the wrong kind, and you find that a little piece of your spirit dies. So consider: What are you doing for "free" or "freely" that is actually costing you? Where have you said "yes" when your body, heart, and soul were saying "no"? What are you believing that you need to question? And are you grieving *your* way, on *your* schedule? Because you can't move *on* after death, you can only move *through*.

2: Things Fall Apart When They Need to Be Fixed

What signs are you getting that an old way of life is ending? Once I was cooking and had a burner on, and I didn't realize that my hand was slowly burning. By the time I noticed, the skin on the back of my hand was bubbling. I managed to cool it down, and the only reason it hasn't scarred is that a colleague told me to liberally douse it in lavender oil!

But how had I not noticed that I was being burned? My mind was so cluttered that I was completely removed from the present moment.

Similarly, around the same time, I kept getting bouts of food poisoning. Often there'd be knots in my stomach, and I'd vomit up acidic digestive material. My body was violently rejecting life at the time. And once I had moved on from that period, I stopped getting unexplained food poisoning.

Exercise: Reflect on Your Situation

What situations are you unable to stomach? Where in your life do you need to be more mindful? Find out by answering the following questions.

1. What slip-ups and accidents have you recently had? What niggling worries, fears, and anxieties are making you disconnected and clumsy?

2. Who or what is causing you to tune out and focus on the past or the future? Who do you need to talk to so you can resolve this? What do you need to say?

3. What have you misinterpreted as anxiety that is actually an appropriate response to a situation or environment?

4. Has sickness reared its head lately? Or has an ongoing condition flared up? What could this be trying to tell you?

5. In what situations do you typically get butterflies in your stomach or a stiff neck? Or shoulder pain? Or other aches and pains? What could these symptoms be trying to tell you?

6. What is the ONE thing you need to do to be more present in your life? (**Note:** this may scare you, but write it down anyway!)

WRITING THROUGH FEAR

While writing the original proposal for this book, I came down with tonsillitis—which lasted for ten days. Now, after having become a longtime student of personal development, I know that physical illnesses also have an emotional / psychological / spiritual component.

In fact, my doctor searched high and low for a reason for my swollen left tonsil but couldn't find one. There were no bacteria, and the typical viruses that cause tonsillitis weren't present. All she could say was that an unknown virus was aggressively attacking my throat. After a week, she got a little worried and ordered more tests. Each one was negative. Nothing was medically wrong.

As you'll have seen, this book is quite personal and full of stories. It's much more personal than my first book *Just Write It!* and pulling it together has been a catharsis. What's more, during the initial writing process, I expressed far more than went into either the final proposal or this book you're reading right now.

I think the flood of emotions swirling around my body had to go somewhere to get out. It's now a medical fact that we store emotions in our cells. And I can't help but think that a hell of a lot were stored in my tonsils.

Throughout those tonsillitis-stricken days, I kept getting flashes of memories. Some were pretty benign, like the amazing leather jacket I bought after graduation from a second-hand shop; some were more unpleasant, like thoughts and feelings about when I felt I was treated unfairly or harshly.

I realized it was fear speaking and that I needed to feel the fear and do it anyway. Fear was rattling round my body like an old knock-kneed skeleton, trying to find its way out. And the only way out for me was to write through it. And then, almost as suddenly as it had swelled up, my tonsil went down. It shrank and shrank, and my throat truly felt better than before. (I tried to explain that to my doctor, but she wasn't having any of it!) Feelings are real, and emotions are energy, and energy has to go somewhere.

If you're going to go deep into emotional writing, your body may cry out in the form of illness or silly accidents. You might stub your toe, slip on a puddle you hadn't noticed, or experience several mishaps as you make sense of or relive emotions that you have stuffed down. This is part of the process; always seek a qualified guiding therapeutic hand if you feel called to do so. Coaches, therapists, psychologists, and psychiatrists all have a role to play in helping us be truly well.

> **So, where in your grief journey are you?**
> **And what do you need to write about?**

Remember that we're all on a continuum of grief. We would not be alive if we hadn't lost. It's an integral part of living. To paraphrase Anatole France: We die to one part of life in order to step into another.

SNAKES AND LADDERS

Now, are there events in your life that seem to happen again and again? Granted, the setting, context, and characters can change. But underneath, is it the same narrative?

If so, it's likely to keep being played out until you learn the lesson. It's like a giant, universe-run game of Snakes and Ladders. Each time you ignore the signs, signals, and serendipities, you go back down the giant snake—sometimes to square one.

So take another look at the two love lessons earlier in this chapter, and consider what signs and signals you may be ignoring in your life. What do they mean? Learn to see your life in metaphors, and you'll see that everything has meaning. We'll look more at this in the next chapter.

> ### One pattern that has pervaded my adult life is unwittingly attracting narcissistic people.

As an empath and a highly sensitive person, I know I'm not alone in this. Narcissists see us as prey—we see them as misunderstood people we can help. It never ends well.

According to the psychologist Stephen Johnson (quoted in an article in *Psychology Today*), a narcissist is a person who has "buried his true self-expression in response to early injuries and replaced it with a highly developed, compensatory false self." Narcissists act as though they are above others, when in reality they are disenfranchised and wounded.

Some just feed off admiration and are brash and obnoxious in the process. Others want to be associated with "perfect" or "special" people. However, some are cruel and calculating. They know exactly when and where to drop emotional bombs that cause people to react. Meanwhile, they survey the damage. Toxic narcissists manipulate people, deliberately telling lies and causing all kinds of crazy behavior. Highly controlling, they can leave people feeling shell-shocked, hollow, and empty. They have zero empathy and don't care about anyone's feelings, even if they initially pretend they do.

Johnson uses the pronoun "he" when describing narcissists, but they're not all men. Roughly speaking, 70 percent are men, and 30 percent are women. I've encountered narcissists of both sexes over and over again. In both personal and professional settings, I'd find myself dealing with the same shizzle. The stress of dealing with these people would end up being too high, and I would leave to seek greener pastures, which were sometimes just as barren.

Now, as an important caveat, not everyone I encountered in work and life was a narcissist. Over the years, I've nurtured lots of relationships with people who were (and are) supportive, loving, and kind. That includes my husband, brother and sisters, family, close friends, and the people I actively welcome into my life.

But, oh boy, was it ultimately an unmanageable pattern. This Snakes and Ladders pattern, though, didn't miraculously appear once I'd graduated and started job hunting. That's just when I began to consciously notice it. In fact, it started in my childhood, and it festered as self-doubt.

When I entered adulthood, I couldn't make sense of all the bullying, domineering people I was encountering. When I looked for reassurance and explanations from some of the people around me, I was often told (depending on who I asked) that it was my fault. If only I could have been more X, Y, or Z, then the abusive person wouldn't have behaved that way. For instance, I've been told to be more vulnerable, hardworking, understanding, patient, and loving. It's all dangerous blah, blah, blah designed to keep the narcissist on top—and it has nothing to do with love, at least not a healthy definition of love. Alternatively, I was told that that's just how life is, and that I had to be a victim and accept it. Tellingly, though, when I confided in healthy, self-confident friends, they quickly set me straight, saying that I didn't deserve to be treated like that and I ought to rectify the situation immediately.

This all continued until the grand old age of thirty-two, when I broke the pattern. It was the morning after a particularly unpleasant incident. It's one that is unfortunately etched in my brain, but I'll spare you the details. Suffice it to say that it culminated in a vicious verbal attack from a friend of a friend.

We were all staying in a hotel in a town I'd never visited before. The morning after, I got up at the crack of dawn, desperate to escape and get some fresh air. The streets were eerily silent, and there was barely anyone around. Yet strangely, that felt comforting. I replayed the events in my mind and suddenly found myself silently repeating, "I love and accept myself, I love and accept myself," until I stood in the street and actually said the words out loud. It wasn't the first time I'd said those words, but this time they reverberated around my body. I truly believed them.

Life truly began to change at, and after, that moment. I raised my standards and began to protect myself against abusive people. I started to get clear on exactly what I would and would not tolerate from others. It wasn't a magic wand, but I began to see life through the lens of someone who loved and accepted herself. I could finally see the behavior of certain people for what it was. Their pathology and their crazy way of engaging with the world and the people in it had *nothing* to do with me, *unless* I engaged with it.

Of course, I still encountered narcissists, and sometimes I unconsciously went back to old ways of behaving. But my breakthrough meant that when I felt the old feelings, I could work through them. I could recognize what was happening and force myself to choose a healthier emotional and practical response. Plus, I simply refused to let any narcissists enter my inner circle.

Don't Suffer in Silence

To be honest, I didn't want to write this section of this book at all. Although these emotions are all processed and safe to share, at its core, this pattern makes me feel vulnerable. But I bit the bullet for two reasons. Narcissists and other abusive people rely on your silence and the shame you feel as a result of their actions. By not speaking out, I would just be perpetuating the silence, which would help no one.

This book is about speaking up—initially via writing—and shining a light on shame, which cannot survive except in the dark. I hope my words help you uncover the pattern that's held *you* back in your life, and that, by shining a light on my experience, I enable you to shine a light on yours.

Write through it, live through it, but above all bring it into the light so that you can see it for what it is. Things always seem more frightening in the dark. At least in the light, you know what you're working with. And shame is not so good at surviving in the sunlight. She's a little like a vampire and turns to dust when the natural light is too bright.

So if you're worried about feeling even more ashamed after confronting what is REALLY going on, know that the shame festers in the dark. By hiding and being small, you are making it continue, and you are planting it further and further down into your psyche.

Finding Strength in Vulnerability

This chapter is about making meaning in dark times and finding a chink of light in the depths of despair. And as such, it is important to highlight that your vulnerability may lead you to being attacked by narcissists and other abusive people. Remember that the best way to protect yourself is to love yourself fiercely.

Take a look at who is with you on your grief journey, and make sure they really deserve to be there. Make sure they are adding to your life and not taking away from it. Process how and what you feel in your journal, and keep it private. You never have to take quick action in the world, but never delay in protecting your heart and soul from damage. Keep listening, and keep your journal by your side.

CHAPTER 7

METAPHOR–THE LANGUAGE OF THE SOUL

So in a practical sense, how can we truly bring shame to light? How can we give a voice to the voiceless? How can we make sense of the gnawing aches in our stomachs? It might sound a little trite, but using metaphors can make a world of difference.

Our experience of the world is perception-driven. If you change your perception, you attribute a new meaning to something that remains unchanged. Your eyes freshen, your ears perk, and you can look at things differently. Whatever meaning you attribute to a thing, whether positive or negative, metaphors give it a chance to really grow legs. And we need that, because in tough times, positivity can be fleeting. It's easier to remember the crap—easier to feed and water the pain. It's harder to feed and water the buds of creative awakening.

The trouble is that it's the unconscious that truly controls how we think and feel, and it holds a storehouse of untold tales. These live deep in the body, in the breath, in the cells, in the seat of our being. The unconscious (or the soul) speaks in images, fragments, and fleeting memories. Memories held in the cells. Ancestral lineage. Hidden trauma. Wounds. Joy. Primal screams.

Metaphors are all about images, fragments, and finding words to convey what is really being felt deep down. There's a reason why

Jose Ortega Y Gasset said, "The metaphor is the most fertile power on earth." Metaphors can help us to make sense of seemingly irrelevant events in our lives. When you actively look for the metaphor, you start to see the deeper meaning in what's *really* going on. And as the poet Muriel Rukeyser said, you'll see that the world isn't made of atoms, it's made of stories.

Becoming truly comfortable with metaphor is transformative. This is because it means that you have developed a whole new language in which to express yourself. And that language will come from the soul—giving you a fighting chance of accessing your unconscious.

THE POWER OF CREATIVE CLASHES

When I was studying for a lyric writing diploma at Berklee College of Music, we played around with metaphors A LOT, because they are the heart and soul of songs. They can hit you in the gut as they are so rich with imagery and meaning. During the course, we'd be given a noun, such as "faucet" or "city," and then would be instructed to find another noun that would make an interesting collision with it. So for example, I would pair the word "heaven" with "faucet" and write: "Heaven's faucet turned on full blast." Or I'd pair up "city" with "sullen" and write: "The sullen city sulked and moaned from the weight of its inhabitants."

The idea was to keep clashing and practicing pairing words until the process of making metaphors was not only fun, but increasingly natural to do. The object writing you practiced earlier in this book will naturally help you to create metaphors. But playing with words in this way helps you go one step further and can be more revealing than you think.

In a lyric writing course with more than a dozen people, we all created very different metaphors, despite having been given the same prompts. In one exercise, I played around with the words "goodbye" and "shame." I wrote, "Her sweet shame was treacle, edging its way down her throat," and, "Goodbye arrests his mind and holds it hostage." We never really critiqued one another's work but merely reacted to the metaphors and shared what we liked. The end result was reams and reams of raw material that we could turn into song lyrics. But for me, I always saw the exercises as being personal development tools in their own right. And for me, the end result was freedom—the freedom to express myself and to share that with my classmates.

Exercise: Create Some Word Clashes

So, now it's over to you. Below is a list of nouns. Brainstorm some other nouns that clash with these and write metaphor sentences like the examples above.

Diary

Pen

Shark

Tattoo

Motorbike

Raincoat

These words are just a suggestion, so feel free to use whatever words you like, and have fun with your word clashes.

SO, WHAT IS YOUR LIFE TRYING TO TELL YOU?

I'm not a long-distance runner, and even at my most fit, when I was a teenage champion sprinter, I could barely make it around a cross-country field in one go. I could do a fast sprint at the end, though! Then I found myself a running buddy who wanted to do long-distance running. I was willing to give it a go. But I tried to explain that as a natural sprinter, I have fast-twitch muscles, while natural long-distance runners have slow-twitch ones. But she said that if I just tried hard enough, if I put all my focus and dedication into it, I could override my natural tendencies and force myself to become a good, slow-and-steady, long-distance runner.

So, I tried. But by putting myself in a box—and the wrong box, at that—I just got frustrated. And not particularly fit either, as my body responds much better to high impact interval training (or HIIT, as it's also known).

What I actually needed to do was harness my anger to shout out about the craziness of what I was putting myself through. For me, putting my head down and working harder simply masked what I was feeling. And at the time, I didn't realize that my anger was a tool—a trusted friend that could tell me where in life I was going wrong.

And that's the thing. We're here to write for creative self-expression and to express our feelings, but sometimes we have no idea they're even there—especially if they're masked by pain and fear and hidden beneath metaphor.

Anger and pain are most definitely linked. In an article in *Medical Health News*, Wyatt Redd explained how fibromyalgia is linked to childhood stress and unprocessed negative emotions. In fact, in 2010, the *European Journal of Pain* reported a study comparing female fibromyalgia sufferers who expressed anger versus those who repressed their anger. The greater the inhibition of anger, the greater the pain experienced by women with fibromyalgia. Those who got angry (and expressed it then and there) experienced the least amount of pain.

If your pattern is to stuff emotions down, whether through food, shallow breaths, or feelings of deep resentment, your challenge is to feel your body in a way that you have never done before. Get it up and out, and get the words into your consciousness. The exercise below might be just the ticket.

Exercise: Collecting the Words That Make Up Your Life

Think about some words that reflect moments and situations in your life. What do you do on a day-to-day basis that drains you? Write that down. What is your experience with exercise, or with your partner, or your friends? Write that down. What is the word or object you associate with visiting your local coffee shop? Write that down. Collect the words, phrases, and names of things that make up the fabric of your life. For a Londoner, this could be the Tube, noisy pubs, and endless crowds. For health and wellness lovers, it could be yoga, breath work, and smoothies.

You could also do a bit of digging into your past for the words and phrases that have firmly stuck with you. For instance, for most of my early life, I got used to people not being familiar with the twin Caribbean islands of St. Kitts and Nevis, where my dad and his family are from. But once, when I tentatively asked a colleague if she was familiar with them, she snapped back: "Of course I am.

Where do you think I've been? Up a frog's bottom?" Nearly twenty years later, these words are still with me. They are so crazily specific and horribly sarcastic!

Another word that can be triggering for me is "stolen." I've had it bandied about by people who don't believe in abundance and who genuinely think that my being given a job or an opportunity is taking away or stealing from them personally.

This attitude is the basis of the entire social media comparison culture—the perception and belief that someone sipping Mai Tais in Hawaii on Instagram has stolen your ability to do the same or the belief that they have somehow used up the resources, network, and support available to do so, and have drained the pool because of it, leaving nothing left for you.

So collect your words, and we will use them to create metaphors. Sometimes the meaning of something is so obvious when you look at it in the clear light of day. Other times, you need to do a little digging, and I will show you a tool for doing so.

A Metaphor-Making Tool

This method of metaphor-making was created by Pat Pattison, a songwriting professor at Berklee College of Music. Here's how to do it. You take your word, phrase, object, or thing and ask yourself two questions:

1. What qualities does it have?

2. What else has those qualities?

So, let's take the word needle, for example—if you're a nurse (or a crafter), this is likely to be a daily staple of your life. Some of the qualities of a needle are: sharp, dangerous, metallic, thin, long, useful, and essential. Then take each of those words in turn and ask yourself: What else is sharp? What else is dangerous? What else is metallic? And so on. The words I came up with were: steeple, iceberg, coin, winter road, paper, and water.

Here are the words arranged in a table to make them easy to see:

Word, phrase, object, or thing	What qualities does it have?	What else has those qualities?
Needle	Sharp, dangerous, metallic, thin, long, useful, essential	Steeple, iceberg, coin, winter road, paper, water

For each column, you can brainstorm as many words as you like. The idea is to first get a full list of words for column two, and then explore each word in full in column three. Finally, you choose a word from column three to describe column one in order to create your metaphor.

So, for example, I could write: "The needle was an iceberg," OR, "The fragile needle was a curved winter road."

As you'll see, it's likely that you'll need to add in other descriptive words so that it makes sense. But this exercise trains you to see things differently. To see a needle as being a winter's road—it's gymnastics for your metaphor muscles.

Exercise: Create Three Metaphors of Your Own Using These Kinds of Tables

The idea is to do these tables without overthinking. So be playful and have fun. However, also be aware that the metaphors you create may be trying to tell you something. We are the product of our thoughts and feelings, and this is a way of bringing them to the surface. So do this exercise when you have a little time and space, and prepare for some turbulence.

A POTENT POWER

Metaphors are at the heart of poetry, and poetry is a potent power. For centuries, it has been used by shamans and witch doctors to promote health and well-being. In fact, in ancient Egypt, words were written on papyrus and then dissolved into a solution so that the words could be physically ingested by the patient and take effect as quickly as possible.

I recently went for lunch with a friend who's a general practitioner, and she gave me an insight into the steady stream of people who come to her doctor's surgery each day. She told me that *so* many people complain of being busy and overwhelmed and that they want a pill to solve this. Some even come back every few weeks because they feel unwell. But it's more that there are layers of niggling anxieties, waves of grief, and emotions which have been packed down and neatly stored away. And there's no fast fix for that. Often, they try counseling and then say it "doesn't work." They present with a cry of the heart and soul, rather than anything that conventional medicine can solve.

Poetry can help you express the more soulful or personal things that you have unwittingly been avoiding. And once you unlock the poetry within you, it'll not only impact your well-being, but will have a positive effect down the line on the rest of your writing. In poetry, the words sing, they come alive, and they jump off the page. They demand to be read, and to be heard, and they invite people to listen. And when creativity is flowing freely, poetry naturally emerges.

Exercise: Find Some Poetry Prescriptions

The good news is that you don't have to do all the hard work yourself. For centuries, poets and songwriters have put into words the things we find difficult to express. And most of us love this. Just think about it: when you hear live music and get taken on an emotional, transformative journey—it can leave indelible marks on your soul. In a similar way, so can reading the words and lyrics of great poets.

If you're not a fan of poetry, I'll hazard a guess that you've been scarred by an over-zealous schoolteacher who told you that literature was something penned by a chosen few and that the only poems worth reading were by people you had nothing in common with.

Seek out rappers and dub poets, spiritual seekers and fashionistas. Seek out voices that connect with you. Go to the library or do an #instapoet search and find a body of work you connect with. Read it, savor it, and let it help *you* express the unexpressable.

When I worked as an English tutor, primarily for high school students in the mid-to-late 2000s, I used to love helping my students to analyze poems in preparation for their literature exams. And the depth of feeling that was in the poems would tap into something in each of us. To this day, the war poem "Dulce Et Decorum Est" by Wilfred Owen still haunts me a little. And that's the point. So don't just give poems a scan read. Buy them in book form or print them out and underline your favorite words. Think about what they really mean, and really picture the images in your mind's eye. What do they unlock in you? What do they represent in you?

It's well worth doing this, as it will also help to you to become a better overall writer. This is because poems:

* Only say what needs to be said

* Use punctuation and short sentences to highlight key words and phrases

* Have a definite beginning, middle, and end

* Only include the most interesting events

* Are highly expressive

* Repeat key words and phrases for effect

* Make great use of literary techniques

These are all the things that will help your own writing to jump of the page and come alive to you and your readers. What's more, poems and the metaphors they contain straddle different layers of the communication pyramid. This means they can touch both hearts and minds and allow you (and your readers) to feel—deep in your center of your body.

SOME THINGS TO REMEMBER

* Feel all the feelings and work through them. Don't minimize, deny, or blame yourself. See your hurt and pain for what it is and take it seriously.

* Take responsibility for what *you* feel and start from there. The end result ought to be lightness and greater well-being, not growing hatred or rage.

* What do you need to write about to heal and to truly love yourself?

* There are *so* many layers of conditioning that we all operate from—don't be afraid of what comes up.

* Faking it until you make it is fine, but it doesn't get you feeling great inside. You need to rebuild from the inside out, not the outside in.

* Get to know your armor. For some, their armor is their makeup, or a certain style of dress. So, you may willingly leave a job in the city—but then find that you've stripped off your armor and have to deal with the world from a very different place. The status is just gone. Your whole identity might need to be reshuffled.

* Focus on cultivating radical self-belief, and use it to gradually replace fear, shame, and embarrassment.

Remember that working with creativity as I'm suggesting you do in this book is a choice, and it has nothing to do with talent. It's about the decision to matter in your life, and consequently in your relationships, at work, and in everything you do. It's been estimated that while 90 percent of five-year-olds are creative, only 2 percent of adults are. Positioning yourself in this creative 2 percent will give you an edge in everything you do.

The World Economic Forum has compiled lists of the top ten skills that people need at various moments in time. In 2015, creativity was number ten; in 2020, it's predicted to be number three. And I predict that creativity will continue to become more and more important. Technology can do so much for us, but it can't help us feel, truly live, or truly be content. It can't help us solve problems of the heart and mind.

I want you to know that you *are* stronger after overcoming setbacks. Research has shown it. And with metaphors and all the other tools in this book you can re-frame, re-name, re-live, re-form, and re-love. You can be *stronger*, *better*, and *brighter*.

PART 3

YOUR LIFE, YOUR RULES

CHAPTER 8

WHAT DOES IT REALLY MEAN TO BE SELF-EXPRESSED?

If you've been following along with the exercises so far, and waking and shaking up your life, people *will* notice. And as with anything new, if you've just experimented a little with the flames of creative desire (but haven't yet managed to master them), they can feel more frightening the longer they burn. Instead of feeling warm and inviting, these flames can seem full of danger—like a bourgeoning bush fire.

Creativity comes from a desire to express your TRUE self. And doing so can feel unfamiliar to you and others. It's unsettling, perhaps even threatening, to see someone rise. The people around you will have to adjust. But it's likely that their first instinct may be to try to douse your flames—thinking you are out of control. They may be scared you're going to burn out, reduce yourself to cinders and char them in the process. They may just think that something is wrong with you and that you must change your ways. But this fire in your heart and belly is a sign that the terrain has changed, and ultimately it means that they need to wake up and shake up too.

All of this destabilizes the status quo. Someone who was once super easygoing and happy to plod along may now need space and time to paint, draw, or sew. Someone once happy to suppress niggling doubts about a situation may feel compelled to speak up. Someone once happy to veg out in front of the TV now needs to journal their thoughts.

Of course, none of these activities in-and-of-themselves are dangerous or threatening. But they are problematic for the people who were invested in your silence and who relied on you to defer to their needs. Not their emotional needs, but their ego needs. The things they rely on other people to give them that they can't give themselves. These are things like attention, care, and nurturance—that they haven't learned to provide for themselves from within. So with your focus on a creative activity, they may feel bereft.

The fact is that these flame-dousers are often unable to see themselves for who *they* truly are. They may seem quite contrary and brash—but that doesn't mean they're self-expressed. Often the most outwardly confident people are the one who wear the most ornate confidence masks. You'd never know they were there until you start developing your own inner core of unshakeable self-belief. Then you realize that their mask was see-through, and you can't quite believe you hadn't noticed before.

This true self-expression isn't the domain of a chosen few. It is everyone's birthright. And if you have to ruffle a few feathers along the way—I say, so be it. Having said that, you need to tailor-make this new self-expressed you so that it fits into your life and complements the things you already hold dear. In short, there's no need to throw the baby out with the bathwater. There's no harm in giving the people around you the reassurance that "you've got this," and "you're all good," and that you're following a path to self-expression that many people have trod before. And you're still there but are just stepping into a fuller, more unabridged version of you. And that, actually, if things get a little shaken up, then no worries. Seasoning a piece of meat, fish, or tofu by shaking it in a

bag before it goes in the oven looks messy, but once it's cooked—
it's perfection!

So this chapter is about getting a little perspective. It's about
exploring exactly what a self-expressed life looks like to *you*. I'll
take you through a series of guided questions, and then you'll map
out a self-expressed day in detail. The aim of this is to show you
that self-expression is a way of life, and when you treat it as such,
it's far easier for your writing (and your life) to flow.

But before we go into detail about what a self-expressed day (and
life) looks like to you, let's look at the benefits of living and loving
this way.

BEING SELF-EXPRESSED HELPS YOU TO CUT THROUGH THE NOISE

I'm the biggest magazine addict out there—but sometimes we need
to stop flicking through pages, or downloading apps, or scrolling
through Instagram, or whatever your media tranquilizer is. If our
outlook is too media-led, we can find it hard to hear our own voices.
We make fun of celebrities who vent their angst publicly. But don't
we all secretly wish we could do this too? That we could bypass the
filters that sometimes make us swallow our own words?

BEING SELF-EXPRESSED HELPS TO GIVE YOU BREATHING SPACE

Carving out the time to be creative requires space, air, and solitude.
And quite frankly, that gives you that all-important "me time." A lack
of creative flow can cause you to overeat, overdrink, and do other
things to excess. By putting yourself first, you won't necessarily

achieve balance, but you can *feel* more balanced, which is perhaps just as important.

BEING SELF-EXPRESSED TURNS YOUR BULLSH*T-O-METER UP HIGH

Now, this is a good thing! It means that you may no longer be able to tolerate people, things, and behaviors that you used to readily accept in your life. But you'll begin to take ownership of your life. So, let's look at how a fully self-expressed day would play out for you.

Grab a Notebook and Answer the Following Questions:

1. When do you find that you reach for mindless activities, such as aimlessly scrolling through social media or snacking when you're not hungry? What are the trigger points for these?

2. What time of day do you have the *most* energy? What time of day do you have the *least* energy?

3. If you could plot out your day exactly as you liked free from *any* responsibilities, what time would you wake up and what time would you go to bed?

4. Assuming you had no responsibilities in the mornings, what would an ideal morning routine look like to you?

5. Similarly, assuming bedtime was whenever you liked and free from any stress or need to wake up at a certain time, what would your bedtime routine look like?

6. What are your favorite creative activities? Dream big here and jot down anything and everything.

The idea of these questions is to begin to see when you are most naturally energized and what kinds of activities you'd do if you had all the time and space in the world. Pretty much from school days on, our lives are mapped out and activities are squeezed into a nine-to-five schedule—give or take a couple of hours. We forget that we're all unique and by forcing ourselves to use our best hours doing the things that bring little joy, we're missing out on our vital energy. So, think about what time you feel most alive, and see if you can create a day around having that as a sacred creative time for self-expression. There'll need to be juggling, compromises, and maybe a complete overhaul of how you view your time. But the first thing is to just become aware.

Think about the time you have en route to places, at lunchtime or on the way home. Are you using this time to feed your self-expression? Where could you take pockets of alone time to think, breathe, and perhaps do a bit of object writing? When are you staying awake with a glass of wine, when, actually, an earlier bedtime would give you some sacred morning time? It's not about making massive leaps just yet, it's more about becoming aware of what you're actually doing and how you're actually living. There is no norm—it's a myth. We're all quite individual people with individual preferences, and, when we realize this, we see we can have a lot more choice and control over things.

Exercise: Plotting Out a Day in Your New Self-Expressed Life

So now, let's look at a current day in your life—either a weekday or a weekend, whichever you prefer. I'd like you to map out every tiny little thing that you can do for your self-expression at different parts of the day: everything from singing a little song in the shower at seven in the morning (or four thirty, if you're a super early bird), to slicing banana onto your porridge; taking a walk where you do a little object writing (or tap ideas out on your phone) to setting aside an afternoon to do some crafting, photography, or writing. Big or small—map out below what this perfect day would look like in hourly increments.

Use the following headings:

* Time
* Activity
* How I feel

This exercise can lead to lots of breakthroughs. As my client and friend Polina wrote, "I find it very hard to make time for anything creative or playful—and have always been this way. My only creative activity is writing, which I do daily and no longer feel guilty about. But I would love to do things like photography, mooching around museums, leisurely city walks, and slow cooking. I shall make an effort to put time in my week for this! Even if it means feeling guilty at first…"

Just like Polina did, I challenge you to incorporate these activities and ideas into your days as much as possible, and then keep refining what you do so that it feels good to you.

Another client, Salma, has told her husband that she needs him to take their daughter on Saturday afternoons so that she can go to a café and write. It sounds so simple, but she had never done this before, despite writing being so important to her. Janine is planning on taking a seven-hour solo train ride from Oslo to Bergen to give her time and space to write, while Rosi has realized that being retired means that she needs to create boundaries and structure in order for her creativity to thrive. It's only when you look at it from a point of view that your self-expression is non-negotiable that life suddenly seems moveable. What once appeared to be made of glass is actually made of play dough and can be molded to suit the needs of your heart and mind.

SOME PERILS ALONG THE SELF-EXPRESSION PATH

Mapping out your ideal self-expression day is one thing, but I DO understand that the real world is much bumpier and that you'll have to constantly remind yourself of your priorities, your intentions, and what's most important to you. Here's a little story about how other people can derail your best intentions—and how you have to be vigilant.

In 2011, my husband and I lived in Ethiopia for three months while we were on a sabbatical working for a charity. On one of my first days of work in Addis Ababa, a colleague took me for lunch and gave me a stark warning. He told me that being a journalist was one of the most dangerous jobs you can do there. He then relayed a list of the people he knew who had fallen afoul of the law. I had actually intended to contribute to some Ethiopian newspapers and had loosely thought I could set up some kind of blog. But the thought of legal trouble, well, that scared me right off.

Now, I don't know if I was supposed to take all of this with a grain of salt. I don't know how accurate all this was. But what I do know is that he was super successful in shutting down my self-expression.

It was 100 percent the right choice for me in that situation. But the trouble is, on reflection, I've received A LOT of other similar warnings. Once in a business mastermind session, long after I left Ethiopia (and in fact, in Norway), the conversation turned to branding. I shared how I was branding my business as me, Greta Solomon, because I'm the one who leads my coaching calls and workshops and writes the books and materials. Another man proceeded to tell me how "dangerous" that was and that no one wanted to hear from me (not on a personal level, anyway) as I wasn't famous.

If you're reading this book, of course you know that's rubbish. I'm sure you could happily reel off lots of personality-driven entrepreneurs from Oprah to Ellen. And yes, they are famous, but they weren't *born* famous.

So how do you know if someone is silencing your self-expression out of kindness and care or because it threatens them personally in some way? It all comes down to the judgement and perspective you gain from committing to a self-expressed life. And don't think for one minute that you and your voice aren't powerful. In the community you live in, in your family, in your work, your voice can carry immense weight—especially if it's leveraged somehow, for instance, by joining a campaign or by being picked up on social media. Silence is control, and speaking up is power. In stifling your words—you stifle your power.

Going from Ethiopia to living in Norway pretty much straight away (from one alien place to another) was a huge psychological hit for me. As a professional writer, it would have helped immensely if I'd documented my feelings, either in a blog or in magazine articles. But the fact is I was apprehensive. I'd already been warned off, and I felt hesitant in putting my feelings down. It was all too much to have to sort and sift through. But I *did* journal, and that made all the difference.

Being self-expressed means that in the midst of chaos and confusion, and fear and uncertainty—there is a creative place you can go where you can rest, somewhere where you can speak without fear of reproach so that nothing you say is censored. There is a place where you can just be confident in who you are and not feel that you *have to* make yourself smaller or bigger than you are.

Chapter 8: What Does It Really Mean to Be Self-Expressed?

It's about being just who and what you are without worrying about reproach—even if you've spent a lifetime training yourself to worry about that. It's about shining in the limelight without worrying about anyone else being in the shade, because each person is in control of their own spotlight, and it's not up to you to turn theirs on or dim yours to make them feel better.

That's why self-expression is so powerful. It's an "on" switch that can light you up in a way that is both powerfully healing and full of goodness. Being self-expressed is about feeling good in a deep way—even when you're silent. Even when you're not writing, or singing, or drawing, or crafting, the intention and the power are still there, bubbling beautifully under the surface.

This way, the part of you that was starving is no longer hollow and empty. When you feel full in this way, it stops you from looking for others to fulfil you, complete you, and make up for your so-called deficiencies. You feel whole and complete as you are. You can stand up and speak up for yourself. You can show who you *really* are through your work, your writing, and your interactions with others.

CHAPTER 9

LETTING GO AND SURRENDERING

Flashback to 2002. I am walking to work when my legs start shaking—before they give way. I don't know whether it's exhaustion or a panic attack. But I collapse on the fence of a neighbor's garden in tears. I ring my brother, who lives a couple of minutes away, sobbing: "Come and get me, I can't walk—there is something wrong with me!"

At the time, I didn't instantly realize it, but I was being given a clear signal that I was walking in the wrong direction—so much so, that my legs would literally take me no further. My doctor diagnosed stress and signed me off work for a week. And in that time away from my hectic job, my perspective began to shift. There was nothing medically wrong with my legs, they just didn't want to walk me into work that day.

I knew that the job wasn't tenable for me in the long term, that I would have to find something different. I needed to find something that meshed better with me as a highly sensitive introvert, even though at the time I had no labels to tell myself or others that was what I was. I didn't yet know that I was "multi-passionate," or that I preferred an entrepreneurial approach to life and work. I didn't know anything except that you were supposed to go to university and get a good job, at a good company. All I knew is that I had been given a sign, and I trusted that my feelings about that sign would take me down the right path.

Now, imagine if I had ignored the sign—ignored the huge wake-up call and pushed on regardless. So many of us do this until we break down, either physically, mentally, or both. People find themselves burned out and with a whole host of physical ailments that their hearts and minds warned were on the way long before they struck. They either weren't attuned enough to listen or were holding on too tightly to what they had created, or to the life they thought they were supposed to lead. Letting go would have felt like a failure, so they clung on until everything just fell away anyway.

It sounds dramatic, doesn't it? But I'll bet you can think of a personal example, either of yourself or someone else, where this has happened in work, life, or relationships. Because as I touched on in Chapter 2, letting go and surrendering isn't easy. If it was, we'd all be doing it. We'd all be letting go of the ties that bind us, embracing our shadow sides, and having a gay old time. (And yes, *The Flintstones* theme tune was just going through my head)!

A LITTLE ABOUT THE SHADOW SELF

The shadow self is the collection of thoughts, beliefs, and behaviors that we've labeled as "bad" for whatever reason. So it differs from person to person. It's what you see as dark or weak about yourself, and so you feel the need to hide it. And most often, it all happens subconsciously anyway. If I had subconsciously believed that resting and recuperating was "bad" and made me "weak," I would have pushed past the wobbly legs, the tears, the stress and would probably have burned out in a dramatic way. Luckily, my shadow self wasn't telling me that. But it's told me a whole load of other stuff that's gotten in the way of me letting go of the things that don't serve me, and prevented me from instead surrendering to the path life wants to take me on. And I'll hazard a good guess that it's doing the same for you.

Think of the shadow as being what's beneath the masks you wear in day-to-day life. If we don't try to bring it into consciousness, then we'll always be looking for others to fulfil the shadow parts of ourselves.

It's important to note that sometimes you have to keep up the mask if there are bullies or narcissists in the vicinity, because stripping off the mask can leave you feeling vulnerable. Do you remember the scene in the classic movie *Pretty Woman* where Edward Lewis buys Julia Roberts' character a beautiful beige and white polka dot dress to wear to the races? When his smarmy lawyer makes a pass at her, she is furious. Without her street outfit, she feels unable to be the tough-talking, take-no-nonsense character she needs to be to bat off harassers. Clothes *do* make a difference. Makeup does too. Whatever we use to bolster ourselves matters. So does eventually liberating ourselves from these props and crutches, but only *when* and *if* we're fully ready to take the consequences.

When you walk through "ganglands," you don't smile and shake hands with the people—you keep your head down and try to exude toughness. You might change your vernacular to be a bit more like everyone else. But if you can't drop that veneer when you're in the safest of places, then that's when there's some work to do. That's when the mask has become a permanent part of your identity.

It takes a lot of courage to drop the mask. For myself, I had to accept that I was (and am) a highly sensitive person and begin to see this not as a weakness, but as a strength. It's only from this vantage point that I can truly surrender and let go of everything I thought I had to be. I thought I had to be tougher, more outgoing, more forthright, more this, more that, and more, more, more. But I didn't. I had to surrender to what I already was. And my legs, that day on the way to work, were trying to tell me that!

BEING YOURSELF AT WORK

Do you feel that you need to wear a professional mask at work? In the past, the divide between "work" and "home" was pretty concrete. You had a "work" self and a private self, and rarely did the twain meet. But these days, employers are encouraging us to be ourselves most of the time. The key to this is to choose which *parts* of *you* are most appropriate at any given moment. None of us is two-dimensional. We're a veritable smorgasbord of goodies that we can offer up at any given time.

It wasn't always like this, though. When I graduated from university in 1999, there was a period where I didn't quite have the confidence to take the leap into a journalism career. I really wanted to be a journalist, but I had NO experience or training in it and had only written one article for my university newspaper—shortly before I left.

So I signed up with a recruitment agency and spent the summer half-heartedly going for interviews. I had graduated from one of the top five universities in the UK, so I was seen as a desirable candidate for graduate recruiters. One interview was with a large banking institution. The interview was going quite well until the interviewer looked me straight in the eye and painted a picture of what my life would be like if I got the job. I don't remember his exact words, but it was along the lines of:

"When you work here, you're expected to meet strict deadlines and work very long hours. It's not unusual to be here until ten or eleven at night. In fact, you'll spend most of your time here. But that's OK, we have a pharmacist here on site, a gym, and most things you need in life. How does that sound to you?"

I replied, "I think it sounds awful. That's not the kind of place I want to work."

The interviewer looked at me with a mixture of shock and curiosity, and hastily drew the interview to a close. The recruiter was furious. She instructed me never to do anything like that again and to always pretend that everything is fine and that you're super happy with whatever a potential employer says.

But that experience never left me, because I always imagined if I had pretended, and I had gotten the job and thought I could pretend for a bit longer—for the money—and then that turned into days, weeks, months, years of not being myself. Plus, I couldn't understand why the world of work was one where you had to pretend anyway. Why was everyone faking?

And it wasn't just that experience where I got that message. In other jobs and other situations I got the message that who you really are is best left at home. There were times when recruiters would tell me to cut out the bits in my resume where I had done things other than journalism, and times when they said that no one would believe that I could be good at both PR and being a writing tutor, so it was best to leave out everything about my writing tutoring business.

I've learned that this is wrong; the most forward-thinking companies want full, well-rounded people, not robots they can slot into a production line. You're not a robot—despite an educational system that has trained us to think that we are.

In the business writing training work that I've have done over the last ten years (helping people to unlearn the traditional academic and corporate ways of writing), I have seen the effect that trying to be one-dimensional can have. In typical offices, people communicate stiffly and strangely. They write in jargon;

they make things complicated and confusing and often don't write what they mean. Once I go in and teach them tools and techniques to write better, they're gradually able to strip off the layers and be more authentic.

But so many people go through life not really being alive and working in jobs where they have to stuff their true feelings inside. I think that's a problem, and it often stems from fear. It doesn't have to be like this. It starts by expressing who you are each and every day—even if it's just within the pages of your notebook. It's about remembering to do writing that takes you deeper down the layers of the communication pyramid, and not getting bound up by lists, goals, and to-dos that come solely from the mind.

Exercise: Six Not-So-Simple Questions

1. What have been some of your signs and signals? Have you been ignoring them or pushing them away, so that they become a dull sense of anxiety or a constant thorn in your side?

2. What do you use as a mask? This could be anything from drinking too much in social situations to being loathe to leave the house without makeup.

3. What are the little anxieties you harbor in daily life that you don't share with others?

4. What or who would you most like to rid from your life, and why?

5. What do you honestly feel you need to surrender to?

6. What do you ultimately need to let go of?

At drama school, my teachers always used to say, "we need to see the layers" of a character. There's always more going on, often many conflicting things at the same time. Think of letting go and surrendering as being like peeling off the layers of an onion. Use the questions above and the food for thought in this chapter to help you put your dreams, hopes, wishes, and fears onto paper. Use these to help you to resist the urge to put on a straitjacket for fear of looking crazy.

FINALLY, HERE ARE SOME THINGS TO SURRENDER TO (THINGS THAT MOST OF US FIND HARD)

Help: Let other people help you. Accept help when it is offered, and ask for it when you need it.

Sleep: Instead of reaching for another coffee, could you squeeze in a power nap or a few minutes where you close your eyes and just rest?

Bad hair days: Even hairdressers can't avoid them.

Done being good enough: It's easy to feel that you can always be better, faster, more prepared, more "switched on." But getting things done is a skill in itself, and, if you take action, you'll always be moving forward.

Things taking triple time: We always underestimate how long things will take, but giving up doesn't make them happen any quicker.

The 20 percent that just isn't in your control: Maybe it's a lot more than this, but with everything in life, there's only so much we have direct control of. But this zone, the 20 percent space, is where all the magic happens.

Letting go and surrendering is not the absence of fear but is about the courage to show up and risk failure and the willingness to stay open to new perspectives and new ways of thinking, being, and living. Keep writing, and keep using the object writing and metaphor techniques you've learned in this book so far.

CHAPTER 10

CREATING PERSONAL, CREATIVE BLOG POSTS

So far, this book has been about personal sharing, mining your heart and soul, looking for the gems in your experiences, and overcoming the blocks to self-love and true self-expression. We've looked at a couple of writing techniques: namely, object writing and the metaphor-making tool. *But* we haven't dived into the myriad of techniques I usually teach in my workshops and online programs. Among other things, we usually look at literary techniques, which are techniques that draw attention to words, phrases, and sentences in a creative way. They make the writing more interesting and make the events jump off the page. They also help to create pictures in your mind to make you want to read more.

Technique can, indeed, be taught. Technique sits in layer two of the communication pyramid. It's about creative and practical tools, tips, and techniques for clear, concise, and compelling writing. And my workshop and course participants are often blown away at how seemingly simple shifts can impact the quality of their writing. But for now, we'll look at the nuts and bolts of sharing your personal stories online.

Don't get thrown by the term "blog." That's just a handy catch-all term for online social sharing. Think of Instagram and other social media platforms as micro blogs. And ignore the naysayers who pop up every now and then to proclaim that blogging is dead. Yes, podcasts may be the new blogs, but sharing writing online isn't going anywhere.

If you want to go whole hog and create (or hone) a personal, creative blog—that's fantastic. But this chapter isn't about WordPress plugins, fonts, or what pictures to choose. Instead, it's more about putting your heart and soul into the world. It's about using writing to help and transform others, or simply help them feel less alone. And ultimately, I think that is the true purpose of writing for creative self-expression.

The flip side of writing for creative self-expression is that eventually we yearn for a reader. We want to communicate with someone, to be seen and to be heard. And at the same time, we can want to run and hide and not reveal anything at all. It's a constant push-pull dance for many of us. As part of my psychology degree, I studied animal behavior, and I kind of see it like the dances that birds and bees do, prancing, shaking their plumes inviting people to come and look, before ducking away to hide.

It can also be difficult to know how much to share. And just like the push-pull dance of being seen and unseen, we can alternately share too much and too little. My philosophy is that we need to resist the temptation to overshare. We can connect without putting all the pieces of ourselves *out there*. And in doing so, we prevent ourselves from becoming addicted to trading fear, pain, and suffering for likes, comments, shares, and follows.

If a story makes you cry while you're telling it, then I believe it's too soon to tell it publicly. This is quite different from feeling all the feelings while writing and releasing tears through catharsis. And it's also different from feeling nervous to hit publish because you feel vulnerable. *Only you* truly know what's right for you and your well-being.

Once a client came to me for a mini writing coaching session, where we explored her personal story. She wanted to use it in a talk she was giving to an organization the following week. She told me an incredibly personal story that moved her to tears. And then she admitted that she hadn't told it to anyone before—not even her husband. But yet, she was willing to share it with a group of strangers. I explained to her that I thought the story was too raw to be shared publicly and that she needed to properly process it. And if in the future, she did decide to share it publicly, she needed to first tell her husband and those closest to her, as it was so sensitive and personal.

And that's the thing with intimacy. Sometimes it can be easier to talk to a stranger than the people closest to us. Usually a (non-therapist) stranger who won't hold you accountable. They won't really unpick the issues, and there's virtually no chance of them now viewing you in a different light. A stranger doesn't know you anyway, and so judgement is often suspended.

Once, at a blogging conference, I saw two women read blog posts aloud that made them cry. Their emotions were incredibly powerful, and they filled the room. But afterwards, I felt sad for them. I worried for their mental health and about what kind of support they had then and there, when they had just unpicked the scabs that were over their temporary healing. Their reading session was the last item on the agenda before everyone departed for a boat party. And I wondered how safe-footed they would feel, literally floating the night away when they were so ungrounded in their own personal power.

This freeing feeling can become addictive. But it's not real, and I don't believe that it's the true purpose of creative self-expression, as I have been outlining in this book. We've got more work to do than that. Our stories need to be grounded in our lives, because we want to use them to make changes in our lives, not as an escape mechanism before we return to the same humdrum existence.

Chapter 10: Creating Personal, Creative Blog Posts

I read a quote today that really hit home. It said, "If you're tired of starting over, stop giving up." When we don't follow through on our healing journey, we can feel like we're always meddling, always trying to fix ourselves. It's like we're constantly picking at the scab, and this can play out in myriad ways—from people pleasing to unwittingly handing over control of your life choices to others.

The criteria for sharing aren't just about the topic, or how personal it is, or who it involves. It's also about whether you are sufficiently healed to tell it without wincing—so that you don't have to pull off the plaster at all because the skin is healed. There may be a scar, maybe even an angry, red, raw one. But a scar indicates healing, and, for me, that's a great barometer for protecting yourself online.

GETTING TO KNOW YOUR AUDIENCE

The first audience you'll ever write for is *you*. And all the writing you've done so far in this book has been resolutely for yourself. When you start sharing your work, your readers will be a little more diverse. However, it's safe to say that the core people who'll read your work will be people like you.

When you write with readers in mind, they become part of the creative process. Granted, this is an invisible process—it's not like with stage acting or presenting, where the audience can become directly involved. But when you actively think about your readers, you can infuse your writing with far more meaning and intent and ensure that the words land correctly. In this way, your readers can help to shape your work so that is it more vibrant and more readable.

Exercise: Here Are Seven Questions to Consider about Your Readers

1. **Who are my readers?** How old are they? What kind of people are they? Where do they live? What do they do for a living? What are their goals, dreams, and aspirations?

2. **How much do they know about the subject or issues I'm writing about?** If you're a crafter, how familiar are they with your techniques or with the intricacy and effort that goes into making what you make? If they don't know, you need to tell them. We always overestimate how much our readers know, and often we need to simplify things.

3. **How important is my blog post to them?** This will vary depending on the content. If it's not important to them in the grand scale of things, you'll have to work harder to get their attention.

4. **What will readers look for in my post?** Why are they reading your stuff in the first place? What do they most want from you?

5. **What is the most important thing to include?** PUT THIS FIRST. NEVER assume that people will read an entire post. Cut out all the preamble and get to the good stuff straight away.

6. **What type of data or supporting evidence do my readers value?** Do they want social proof, like testimonials? Are they more concerned with what celebrities are doing? Do they want numbers and hard facts?

7. **What do I want my readers to do, say, feel, and think after they've read my blog post?** If you want them to do something you have to tell them. Click here. Check out this fabulous thing I made. Feel—have you allowed them to do this?

Be *bold* in speaking to your readers and in deciding who your readers are. If you want people to *love* you, and if you want to write from the *heart*, you have to be willing to alienate certain groups of people who will not "get" or value you.

OPENINGS AND ENDINGS

As explained at the top of this chapter, the ins and outs of all the writing tools and techniques that you can use to write blog posts are best taught in either an online or live workshop setting. But I'd like to share a technique that can completely transform your writing. And that is to make sure you purposefully craft introductions and conclusions to everything you write. Don't take it for granted that they'll naturally come. Sometimes they do, but most of the time you have to go back and craft one. Often the ending paragraph is actually the most important part and needs to be put at the beginning.

Here are some openings you can use; you can also use these as conclusions, too. Just be sure to mix and match so that you don't open and end with the same technique.

Story: Usually something highly interesting and unusual, this is also called an anecdote.

Statement: A surprising or interesting statement, fact, or opinion.

Fact or Description: A short paragraph describing a person, place, or thing. Can also describe or sum up the past.

Quote: Presenting the words someone has said.

Question: A surprising or interesting question that makes the reader want to know more.

Here's an example of a story opening that I took from a blog post I wrote called "The Creative Crucible of Motherhood." It was a piece about how women need a creative outlet other than family, and the story served as a vivid example of why.

A few years ago, I went out for dinner with a dear friend of mine who's a mum of two young boys. Our plates had arrived, and she proceeded to cut her entire meal into bite-sized pieces. Then she looked up at me, mortified, and said: "Oh my God, I can't believe I've just done that. I'm so used to cutting up food for the kids."

I then went on explain that now that I'm a mum too, I understand why my friend did that! And I know now that the best way to counteract the exhaustion and overwhelm is to tap into a different source of energy. Play around with these openings in your own articles and blog posts, and you'll begin to develop a style of your own.

WHAT TO WRITE ABOUT

Don't overthink or fall into analysis paralysis over what to write. You can and ought to write about anything and everything. It's not an exam, and you don't have to pick a niche or make a business case for what you post. Just write. And make it as trivial or as serious as you like. Can't think of anything? What was the last conversation you had with your hairdresser, best friend, or the lady in the checkout line at the supermarket? Write about that. The things you think and talk about are the things you need to write about.

Here is a non-exhaustive list of topics to whet your appetite.

You could write about your hopes, dreams, fears, feelings, and passions around:

* Work
* Children
* Poverty
* Memories
* Family
* War
* Reality TV
* Celebrity gossip
* Big pants
* Horror movies
* Art
* Education
* Food
* Fashion
* Gardening
* Cars
* Music

In short, write about the things that you are passionate about, *anything* and *everything*. If you don't know what you are passionate about—ask yourself what you're curious about. What puzzles you? Baffles you? Makes you scratch your head in wonder? Follow the path of curiosity, and you'll find yourself in a land of wonder.

WHEN TO WRITE

Write whenever you like. The key thing to know here is that you don't need to be "in the mood," and you don't have to always rely on creative inspiration. Writing can be true and heartfelt even when it's carefully crafted and not divined from the skies.

Creative inspiration is just one way to write a blog post. It's about getting yourself into an inspired state by walking, showering, chopping vegetables, and doing other activities to switch off your conscious brain and activate your artist's brain.

Last year, I went to Vogue House in London to meet the new editor-in-chief of British *Vogue*, Edward Enninful. He had agreed to meet one hundred people to do a meet and greet and sign special hardback copies of his inaugural issue of *Vogue*. For a magazine junkie like me, it was an incredibly exciting experience. That night, buoyed by the amazing day I'd had, a blog post, which I later published in the *Huffington Post*, just flowed out of me. I was in the right state to write an entire piece, which I only had to edit for typos and minor style points later.

A couple of weeks later, a friend asked me what I thought Meghan Markle's then-engagement to Prince Harry meant for black people. She asked me this via email, and by answering her questions, I saw I had the germ of a blog post.

This is another way you can write: by getting someone to ask you questions and then writing down your answers and then piecing them together. You don't even need another person to question you, in fact. Write down the questions that spark your curiosity and then answer them.

The third way of writing is to piece together all the information, thoughts, and ideas you have—a little bit like a jigsaw puzzle. To use this method, you write down everything you can think of in any order and then get a pair of scissors and cut up all the sections. And then you piece them together based on how you think they best fit. Get some sticky tape and play around with this. You can also color-code all the similar sections so that you find it easier to find which bits need to go where. So if you were writing about leadership at work, you could color-code all the facts in orange and all the examples in green, and then the quotes in blue—and so on. In my online course, we go further than this with my building blocks method of writing articles and blog posts. There are four universal building blocks and ten mix-and-match ones that make up pretty much all documents. Learning these, along with some key structural rules, gives you an effective container for your creativity.

Staying inspired, though, is definitely helpful in this journey, no matter what method you use. I also feel that when inspiration strikes, it's often nice to share that thought on social media pretty quickly. That light of inspiration can infuse the post with more energy and power if you do it right away. For me, it sometimes feels as though that information was meant to be shared then—and it will land best if it's consumed hot right away rather than cold, days (or even weeks) later. This is not meant to put pressure on you at all, though. It's more about taking advantage of quick posts that can keep your creative juices flowing AND connect with your audience at the same time.

WHY YOU SHOULD WRITE

Well, why not? Through writing you can vent (a little), love (a lot), and share (whether good or bad). It's a strange thing being a writer. There is something magical about seeing your name in print next to something you have written. And it's a magic I never tire from. It's as though by writing (and publishing), you are saying, "I am here. Look! I have arrived. I have a contribution to make."

Often, it's a quiet contribution, but sometimes you'll get lots of voracious readers who will spark a conversation. And this is where I think many of us fall down. We're afraid of the comments, afraid of being spammed, ridiculed, or shot down, afraid of how people may react. And if this is you? Simply turn off comments. You can do that for almost *every platform* until you feel comfortable. And of course, if you have a blog, invest in anti-spam software to weed out the bots.

But if you keep going, there'll come a time when you start (or continue) to build up a community of readers you know, like, and trust—and vice versa. This happened to me, and when a fellow blogging friend complained that she couldn't leave a comment on a particular blog post—I knew it was time to switch on my comments and start having conversations.

The act of putting your words out there is amazingly transformative. Each time you share, you grow just a little bit more. And if you're a professional writer, having a personal blog can support your career.

For me, a blog is a boat that a writer can rest in as they navigate the choppy seas. Magazine pieces may be killed, or that amazing start-up where you worked as a writer may suddenly go under, leaving your invoice unpaid. But if you have a personal creative blog—essentially, it'll be for you. Sure, people will read it, but it's your agenda, free from editorial or style guidelines. You are the editor-in-chief, the publisher, and the content creator. And, as a writer, it's liberating to have a vehicle that puts you in charge of your creative destiny.

CHAPTER 11

WRITING YOUR OWN LIFE

So if someone found the contents of your journal with all the writing you've done while reading this book—would it accurately reflect your life? I don't know about you, but the mental chatter I record in my private writing is often far removed from what's actually happening in my life. And when I look back at pivotal life moments, the punch-you-in-the-gut feelings I sometimes felt didn't necessarily correlate with my feelings from a holistic perspective. For instance, I may have been sad to leave a job I loved, but at the same time I was excited about the future. Nothing was ever 100 percent one thing—there were always nuances.

Just as what we say or think usually isn't the whole story, neither is what we write. It's all subjective. But with that comes freedom. You can write it and it is, and you can think it and it is. You can decide what the great volume of "letters" that you—as the leader of your life—are going to write will be.

The private writing that records your angst, your pain, and the inner workings of your mind is and always will be a powerful transformation tool. But, in terms of leaving a legacy of writing, the *very life* you are living right now (with all the details you may think are too humdrum to record) is far more *valuable* than you may think.

When I look back, my mind plays tricks. I remember the big sweeping gestures and the major life events. But I forget the everyday, ordinary things: what I ate, where I went, the shoes I wore, and the seemingly (but not) insignificant conversations I had. And it wasn't until recently that I realized how precious these are.

When my friend (and serial expat) Sonia left Oslo to move to Chicago, she spent twenty-one days taking pictures of the day-to-day things she was leaving behind: things ranging from the café that served coffee in bowls to the tram network. Because this was life, and she knew if she didn't take these pictures, she would forget what her life in Norway had *actually* been like. She would forget the steps she trod day in and day out. And so she wanted to give them the reverence they deserved.

The first commandment of Oslo's nineteenth century literary bohemian circles was, "Thou shalt write thine own life." I was an Oslo resident for six years, and it took me a long while to grasp that this was the way forward. But now that I have, I haven't looked back. And writing for creative self-expression is just that: writing your own life. So one of my final challenges to you, dear reader, is to ask this question: Are you truly the author of your own life? If not, how can you write your own story every day? How can you write it inside and out, the mundane and the marvelous, the little and the large, the moments of magic, and the moments of mess, the joy and the pain?

EMPOWERING YOURSELF THROUGH WRITING

My first post-graduation job in fashion PR at the age of twenty-two was always a sore spot for me. I felt bullied and belittled, and I simply didn't fit in the swanky world of high fashion. I was thoroughly uncomfortable for three months before I jumped ship and went on to find a job at a magazine where I *did* fit and where I *did* feel comfortable. For years, just the mere mention of that time and that job made me a little queasy. It was such an incredibly stressful experience.

And then last year, I wrote a humorous and heartfelt article about my experience in that job that I published in the *Huffington Post*. In doing so, I took control of my narrative by transmuting it into something that lived outside the realms of my overactive mind. It was an uplifting piece, and the process of writing and publishing it, and then responding to comments about it, took away the sting. It no longer hurt. My experience had become something outside of me—a piece of art.

This is what I challenge you to do too—to make art out of life and to transmute your stings into something else. I touched on this in the last chapter about writing personal, creative blog posts. And this ability to make art out of life is a key reason why it's vital to give yourself proper time to process things before you write about them. I didn't write about my fashion PR experience until eighteen years after it happened. OK, that example may be a little extreme, but you're not on any deadlines here. Just because our lives are increasingly instant doesn't mean our minds are. Time is a luxury, and processing time is the epitome of time luxury. It gives you space and time to heal and to make the proverbial lemonade out of lemons. And, by doing so, you can transmute your experiences so that they no longer *hurt* you but *empower* you. In doing so, you write your own life.

WHY CREATIVITY IS THE MISSING PIECE IN THE WELLNESS PUZZLE

Way back when quinoa was something that no one could pronounce, creatives knew the inherent benefit in making art.

The anecdotal evidence was clear to see. Creative types who weren't functioning artists tended to go down the addiction route. But if they could make art they could heal. And people have long credited creativity with preventing them from pushing the self-destruct button.

Then the wellness movement came along in all its might. Talking therapies became more mainstream, and the value of diet, exercise, and alternative remedies were finally acknowledged. Yoga, mindfulness, and meditation are now no-brainers, but the importance of art and creativity seems to have fallen by the wayside.

Today, a host of products and services have arisen to make wellness a $3.4 trillion global industry, according to a *Global Wellness Institute* study. That includes healthy eating, nutrition, and weight loss, preventative and personalized health, complementary and alternative medicine, and beauty and anti-aging products and services.

Wellness tourism is booming, and, in our busy world, it's becoming increasingly common to check your phone at the spa door, get pampered and preened, and return to an even busier life.

Unfortunately, the busyness of modern life is stripping our brains of their creativity. Research by the Bar-Ilan University in Israel has shown that we *need* to be bored and idle in order to stimulate our creativity—that we need to be able to switch between focus and daydreaming.

However, many of us simply have no downtime. We're on all day, before crashing into bed. It's a rinse-and-repeat cycle that's damaging mentally, physically, emotionally, and spiritually. If you live like this for too long, your emotional experiences flatten out.

If you get too numb, you feel nothing, and life becomes devoid of passion, purpose, and power.

The problem is that emotions are never benign, and, whether you feel them or not, they are still there. Emotions are living, breathing entities that cause changes in blood chemistry—literally affecting our physical health. And finally, both Western and Eastern doctors are beginning to agree on this. One thing is for sure, stress is responsible for disease. The *American Institute of Stress* estimate that between 75–90 percent of all doctor visits are for stress-related problems, while another study published by the *American Psychological Society* found that 90 percent of adults believe that stress can contribute to the development of major illnesses. We feel it, we see it, we know it. Not to mention the fact that emotions are infectious. If you're hanging out with people who are just as stressed and put-upon as you, you're all going to feed off that shared energy. Your brainwaves will pulse on that beta energy, and that can keep you strung out and stuck.

Beta energy is when you're in fight-or-flight mode. This is common in the corporate world, where success often means putting out fires and dealing with crises. It's about pushing, striving, and achieving linear goals. It's about stress and strain. Getting into an alpha brain state is what this book has been all about. That happens when you're alert yet relaxed. It's the state where you can access your intuition and write, think, and speak freely. The first part of this book was all about finding this creative identity in yourself and using it to forge a path ahead.

PERFECTLY IMPERFECT YOU

My clients often tell me that they have analysis paralysis. They're too perfectionistic and can't bear to let their creative work go until it's perfect. But then they feel sad and ashamed at not fulfilling their potential—because they're not actually putting out work into the world. They look around and see others releasing things they consider ugly, and they know they could do so much better if only they could let themselves shine.

If this is you, then you may also be stuck in other areas. Things such as:

Choosing the wrong guy or girl every time, despite your best intentions or feeling isolated, yet again.

Changing roles or jobs and finding that you're still targeted by an office bully, or simply feeling that you've outgrown your life.

Resolving to work less, drink less, smoke less, eat less or worry less, and finding that no matter the situation, you behave exactly as you always have.

Making sure that everyone else is happy and then wondering why you feel so empty deep down.

Fearing that if you slow down, you'll never pick up the pace again and never really achieve anything.

Trying harder and harder to fulfil other people's ideas of success.

Not putting in 100 percent because you're waiting for your "real life" to start.

Acting like the life of the party, when deep down you know you're a creative, sensitive soul.

These things happen when you aim for perfection rather than being true to yourself. It's as though your psyche knows that you are off-key and sends you more bum notes in the hope that you'll notice too! In fact, I'll bet that it's your smart, talented, and capable manner that is actually holding you back because you sometimes want things to be "just right." I'll bet that you sometimes know exactly what you want but feel afraid to articulate it.

Who do you know who is in this creative zone, or at least is dipping in and out of it? To shake off perfectionism and stay on the creative track, it's vital that you keep the right company. And in this digital age, this is getting easier and easier. Join online communities for people like you and seek conversations with people who are striving for more creativity in writing, work, and life. There are a host of resources, organizations, and communities (including my own) at the end of this book to help you do this. Find people who, no matter where they are right now, are optimistic for the future, who, no matter how dark the tunnel, can see the chinks of light at the end. Start getting to know people who are on the same path as you.

Plus, cultivate the willingness to be a beginner and to do creative tasks badly—especially in the beginning. And always remember that creativity (and writing for creative self-expression) is a remedy. It's a tonic that can help bring about real change by connecting us back to ourselves and others.

There is, however, a caveat when it comes to writing your own life

If you're a spiritual seeker and/or a personal development fan, it's likely that you'll have come across the law of attraction. Put simply, this is the belief that focusing on positive or negative thoughts (and images) can bring positive or negative experiences into your life. You may even be a fan of this law and have marvelled at the goodness you have manifested in your life. I, too, am no stranger to the warm, fuzzy feeling when something on my vision board plays out in real life. So, yes—life can be full of magic and serendipity. And scientists have found that mind influences matter. But the law of attraction is not absolute.

You are *not* responsible for others' maltreatment of you. Wars, slavery, and oppression of all kinds are *not* the fault of the afflicted people. And similarly, if something bad is going on in your life (or has gone on), *you (personally) have not manifested it*, and neither have they. And now, I'm going to say it again for the people at the back. The myriad of things that happen in life are not your fault. And thinking otherwise can lead you down a dark path where you try to be a better or a nicer person. Please do not do this.

Taking responsibility and writing your own life is about keeping your mindset healthy and using that to impact how you feel (and how life feels to you). But it's not a magic wand. The odds in this world are always stacked in favor of certain groups of people. It's a fact that people are routinely treated badly simply because of their gender, sexual preference, color, race, religion, or creed. Life isn't fair, but I'm all about taking charge of what you *can* take charge of: forging ahead, dreaming and doing, and defying the odds. Getting angry is good, but just like the sex transmutation I talked about in Chapter 2, it has to be turned into creativity to have real power.

Challenge: Create a Writing for Creative Self-Expression Circle

Walking in this world, living, loving: it all needs a witness. Writing is *so* powerful but writing in groups has its own special energy. In my in-person writing for creative self-expression retreats, I bring together eight to ten people. We share experiences, fears, hopes, and dreams. We excavate writing blocks. We walk and write. We laugh a lot (and sometimes we cry—because tears are OK too). Sometimes we have a glass of wine and too many potato chips. Other times we stick to cleansing water and juice. We experience the joyful feeling of being able to write freely, all while feeling safely cocooned from the hustle and craziness of our busy lives.

While I do lead online workshops and programs, sometimes you just need to be shoulder to shoulder and eye to eye with fellow writers and creativity seekers. So I encourage you to create your own self-expression circles where you can write your own stories, share your successes, and mine your experiences for the gems they contain. Aim to cultivate what my retreat participant Rosi calls a sense of "gracious generosity." She said, "I feel less alone and more supported since being with you and the wonderful group of writers. Your personal aura, your ambience, Greta, is of generosity of spirit, of clarity, of possibility. It is possible for me to do this." Go with your gut and feel your way into the right spaces, with the right people. Then you can continue to practice the exercises in this book and get valuable help and support from like-minded people.

Exercise: Here Are Some Fun and Freeing Questions to Answer

1. Write your cosmic shopping list—what would you *really* want to be, do, and have if the universe / life were in charge?

2. What are ten unique or interesting things about you?

3. When and where do you feel most seen and acknowledged?

4. What small resentments could you shake off in order to free up some trapped energy?

CREATING A MEANINGFUL LONG-TERM RELATIONSHIP WITH YOURSELF

What comes to mind when you think of "wooing"? You might think of a Victorian lady showing an ankle to her beau, a man bringing his love chocolate and flowers, or perhaps a chivalrous gentleman putting his coat over a puddle for his lady to walk over and not even considering taking her to bed until he has wined and dined her over several weeks, or even months.

The trouble is that in our society, we're used to quick transactions. But a writing life isn't a one-night stand, and I want to leave you with this message. You need to woo yourself and do it with style. Keep your creativity alive, and remember that the surface things you do to feel well may even be the wrong things for you, if you haven't had the time and space to consider what you *really* need. Carving out time so that you can be creative gives you access to the liminal space. That's the space between here and now and the future. And in that space lies the magic of potential and possibility. Through creativity, you can remove yourself from the reality you currently find yourself in. You can unplug from the busyness of life and choose another path.

Wooing yourself isn't just about buying nice things for yourself, or splurging, or indulging in other ways. Creativity isn't a product that you can buy. It's a feeling; an invisible life force. It's the missing piece of the puzzle—and, for this reason, it needs to be a key part of wellness.

If you want to improve your well-being, improve your creative self-expression.

Truly self-expressed people tend to ooze self-love, and they completely accept themselves. And they're usually successful— both personally and professionally. But they had to undergo a creative explosion to enable them to see themselves for who they truly are. And that's what I wish for you.

A (very welcome) side effect of all of this is that it's likely that this creative process will open you up so that you can create what you want to create. This could be a business, a blog, a book, or a brand. Perhaps a community of like-minded people or a spiritual practice or exercise routine you *love* doing. Great friends and fun times. Peace of mind. The man or woman of your dreams. In short—create a joyful life.

But don't expect the creative channel to always be open and flowing. Expect it to chop and change just as the tides and the seasons do. It can't always be summer or spring, and sometimes— no matter how hard you try—the flowers just won't bloom. Accept then that it's winter, and plant as many seeds as you can for a later harvest.

What's more, as you go through life, your interests and your ideas change, and that's how it ought to be. If you don't change, you go backward. So spend time looking, thinking, reading, and walking— not just doing. OR head straight to the beginning of the book and begin again to blast through blocks and shake off the shackles.

Creativity is never dormant, and results, breakthroughs, and insights need to be renewed again and again. Keep walking and writing. Keep loving and living. Keep listening and dreaming. Hold your head high, keep your pen close, and write with heart, sass and soul.

SOME JOURNALING PROMPTS TO TRY, SHARE, KEEP AND REVISIT

What are 10 interesting things about you?

_____

_____

_____

_____

_____

_____

_____

_____

_____

_____

_____

_____

_____

_____

_____

Write out your "cosmic shopping list." Remember, this is your ultimate dream list of things you want to be, do, and have if the universe/life were in charge.

_____

_____

_____

_____

_____

_____

_____

_____

_____

_____

_____

_____

_____

_____

_____

Write about your hopes.

_____

_____

_____

_____

_____

_____

_____

_____

_____

_____

_____

_____

_____

_____

_____

Write about your dreams.

_____

_____

_____

_____

_____

_____

_____

_____

_____

_____

_____

_____

_____

_____

_____

_____

_____

_____

Write about your fears.

_____

_____

_____

_____

_____

_____

_____

_____

_____

_____

_____

_____

_____

_____

_____

_____

_____

_____

_____

What *really* matters to you?

_____

_____

_____

_____

_____

_____

_____

_____

_____

_____

_____

_____

_____

_____

_____

_____

_____

What stands in the way of your creativity?

_____

_____

_____

_____

_____

_____

_____

_____

_____

_____

_____

_____

_____

_____

What are you really passionate about and how can you bring more of that into your life?

_____

_____

_____

_____

_____

_____

_____

_____

_____

_____

_____

_____

_____

_____

_____

What makes you feel blocked and stifled and what can you do about it?

_____

_____

_____

_____

_____

_____

_____

_____

_____

_____

_____

_____

_____

_____

How can you access that deepest part of yourself and write from that place?

_____

_____

_____

_____

_____

_____

_____

_____

_____

_____

_____

_____

_____

_____

What is your personal truth?

_____

_____

_____

_____

_____

_____

_____

_____

_____

_____

_____

_____

_____

_____

_____

_____

What do you see as your life's purpose?

_____

_____

_____

_____

_____

_____

_____

_____

_____

_____

_____

_____

_____

_____

_____

_____

List some of your writing ideas–any and all are OK!

_____

_____

_____

_____

_____

_____

_____

_____

_____

_____

_____

_____

_____

_____

_____

_____

_____

Some Journaling Prompts to Try, Share, Keep and Revisit

What is your writing personality and how does it work best for you?

_____

_____

_____

_____

_____

_____

_____

_____

_____

_____

_____

_____

_____

_____

_____

When do you feel at your most creative? Where do you feel at your most creative?

_____

_____

_____

_____

_____

_____

_____

_____

_____

_____

_____

_____

_____

What truly inspires you? How can you inspire others with your writing?

_____

_____

_____

_____

_____

_____

_____

_____

_____

_____

_____

_____

_____

_____

What truly brings you joy?

Pick one thing from your joy list (from chapter three) and write about it.

_____

_____

_____

_____

_____

_____

_____

_____

_____

_____

_____

_____

_____

_____

_____

What do you most want to share with the world in your writing?

_____

_____

_____

_____

_____

_____

_____

_____

_____

_____

_____

_____

_____

_____

_____

_____

What do you need to write about to truly heal and love yourself?

_____

_____

_____

_____

_____

_____

_____

_____

_____

_____

_____

_____

_____

_____

ACKNOWLEDGMENTS

In early 2016, I needed a break from my business. I had spent four years pitching, developing, creating, and delivering business writing workshops (alongside being pregnant, and then a new mum). And I needed to get back in touch with myself.

I cleared my schedule with the aim of doing nothing in particular. And that's when the yearnings, inklings, and frantic writing began. After years of writing to order, I finally wrote what I wanted to write. At first it was like clearing the phlegm from my writing throat. But soon, the channel was open, and the essence of this book flowed, as did a workshop in writing for creative self-expression, which sold out within hours. I knew I was onto something.

Pretty soon I had the proposal for this book. All I had to do was bring it to life, i.e., get it published, which is easier said than done. So, this letter of thanks is to the people who made that happen, the people whose love, care, and support provided the alchemy to bring these words to life in both print and digital form so that they can effect change in the world.

First things first, I'd like to say a huge thank you to Lee Constantine, the cofounder and chief marketing officer of Publishizer, an innovative crowdfunding platform that connects authors with publishers. I hadn't considered running a preorder campaign before you reached out to me. Your coaching, help, support, and unwavering belief that my campaign would be a success is what led me to land 255 preorders, and subsequently, a publishing deal with Mango Media.

As a traditional, independent publisher that does things in a nontraditional way, Mango is the perfect publisher for me. In fact, after my preorder campaign finished, I had interest from publishers in the both the UK and the US. Mango was the winner in every aspect.

Thank you to my friend and fellow writer, Maddie Lama Sjåtil. The biggest investor in my preorder campaign, she purchased a hundred copies as part of my Hire Me to Speak Package. This turned into us cohosting two transformational writers' retreats at Maddie's luxury cabin in the Norwegian mountains. You are the perfect cohost, and it has been so much fun working together in this way.

Thank you to Salma Shah, who became a Patron of my campaign by preordering twenty-five copies to distribute to her network of coaches, consultants, and changemakers. Thank you to Natalie Trice, author and founder of PR School, and Rachel Ricketts, author and racial justice advocate, who each preordered ten copies as part of the Personal Coaching Package.

Thank you to my PR representative Suzie Bartle, founder of Well Spirited PR, who not only helped me to get featured in the UK media after living abroad for six years, but who also preordered the Bundle Package, As did Amparo Heiman, Antoinette Malonga Caro, Jennifer Lopez, Miriam (Edee) Carey, Reidun Kristiansen, and Nancy Durrell McKenna, the founder and director of SafeHands for Mothers. Thank you, all.

For my other preorder supporters, who bought copies for themselves (and for friends)—thank you. You are too numerous to mention here, but I am thinking of each and every one of you. Thanks also to Cee Olaleye at Hey Is That Me?, Nia Davies at NiaFaraway.com, Tamu Thomas at Three Sixty, Ruby Warrington and Bess Matassa at The Numinous, and Nadine Hill at BritMums for featuring my preorder campaign on your online platforms.

We did it! And I say "we" because this was very much a team effort. And every single preorder and message of support helped to inch me closer to my goal.

A huge thank you goes to Brenda Knight, Director of Acquisitions and Editorial at Mango. You were the first person at Mango to read my book proposal and you have championed *Heart, Sass & Soul* all along. Your support, advice, and guidance have been invaluable. Thank you to the founder of Mango, Chris McKenney, for publishing this book. And thank you to the entire team who have worked so hard to bring this book to life. This includes Elina Diaz, Yaddyra Peralta, Michelle Lewy, Christina McCall, Hannah Jorstad Paulsen, Ashley Blake, MJ Fierre, Alina Perin, Merritt Smail, and Natasha Vera.

Three months before I began my crowdfunding campaign, I met with Abiola Bello and Helen Lewis of The Author School. They encouraged me to finish writing my manuscript and not hang around waiting for things to happen. Thank you, ladies. This advice was invaluable as it meant I had a completed draft manuscript before beginning my campaign, which took away a lot of the pressure. It made me feel I was preselling a book, not just a book idea.

Thank you to my friend Polina Norina, a writer and editor who read through the early drafts of this book. Your feedback and insights were invaluable. Polina also generously did this for my first book *Just Write It!*

That I can successfully live the writing lifestyle is not just my own doing, but also my darling husband's, Krister Kristiansen. From day one, you have staunchly supported my writing dreams and ambitions—and I am so grateful for that. I'm proud to be team Kristiansen, even though I will never lose my maiden (and writing) name of Solomon!

To my dear friends, family, clients, course participants, and all those I've connected with both online and offline, thank you for your support. This book is my gift to you. It is my dearest and deepest wish that this book inspires you as you have inspired me.

SOME RESOURCES

MY WRITING COURSES AND RETREATS

Journey Beyond Journaling, Five-Day Online Challenge

This is a free, five-day writing challenge designed for people who yearn to write more. If you feel your voice has been suppressed in some way—this is the challenge for you. Visit www.gretasolomon. com/challenge to receive daily videos and creative exercises that you can complete in ten to fifteen minutes. These will support you in releasing mindset blocks, getting into your body, awakening your senses, and opening your heart. You'll kickstart your writing and creativity and begin to see what's possible for you—beyond the pages of your journal. You can also join a community of writers through a private Facebook group.

Writing for Creative Self-Expression, Seven-Week Online Program

This is a completely tried-and-true, seven-week course in mindset, creativity, and craft. Using videos, audios, and worksheets, I guide you to break through the blocks that hold you back. Through writing workouts, coaching questions, tasks, challenges, and tutorials, you'll wake up to your writing potential. Plus, you'll learn practical tools and techniques for writing articles and blog posts. By immersing yourself in this material, you'll begin to uncover your voice and learn how to use it. You can also join a community of writers through a private Facebook group.

As Janet McQueen, a blogger and photographer, said, "I really loved this course. Your videos are not only a wonderful teaching tool, but each time I watch them, I feel like we are having a cozy chat in my living room! The course content is extremely useful, well-researched, and professionally presented. I am already writing with a newfound confidence and enthusiasm, and I know I will use your tools and techniques as long as I write, which I hope will be forever." Find out more about this unique, life-changing program here: www.gretasolomon.com/online-course.

Heart, Sass & Soul In-Person Writers' Retreats

My weekend-long writers' retreats are a chance to get back in touch with you and your inner writer and spend time stoking the creative flames alongside like-minded people. The retreats are a mixture of practical talks and workshops, walking and writing, private writing time, personal coaching, and powerful intention setting. You'll see that you're not alone and that all writers struggle with the same discouraging thoughts and issues. What we do to overcome these, and how we do this, is what matters. **Hint:** It's all about grace, humor, compassion, and understanding.

More details at www.gretasolomon.com.

MY FAVORITE BOOKS

Writing

Alma, Deborah, *The Emergency Poet: An Anti-Stress Poetry Anthology* (Michael O'Mara, 2015)

Fry, Stephen, *The Ode Less Travelled: Unlocking the Poet Within* (Arrow, 2007)

Jepson, Jill, *Writing as a Sacred Path: A Practical Guide to Writing with Passion and Purpose* (Celestial Arts, 2009)

Pattinson, Pat, *Writing Better Lyrics: The Essential Guide to Powerful Songwriting—From Ideas to Developing Verse and Beyond* (Writer's Digest Books, 1995)

Maisel, Eric, *A Writer's Paris: A Guided Journey for the Creative Soul* (Writer's Digest Books, 2005)

Creativity and the Creative Process

Brackney, Susan M., *The Lost Soul Companion: A Book of Comfort and Constructive Advice for Black Sheep, Square Pegs, Struggling Artists, and Other Free Spirits* (Dell Trade, 2001)

Gilbert, Elizabeth, *Big Magic: Creative Living Beyond Fear* (Bloomsbury Publishing, 2016)

Henry, Todd, *Louder Than Words: Harness the Power of Your Authentic Voice* (Portfolio, 2015)

Tharp, Twyla, *The Creative Habit: Learn It and Use It for Life* (Simon & Schuster, 2006)

Smith, Keri, *Living Out Loud: An Activity Book to Fuel a Creative Life* (Chronicle Books, 2003)

Personal Development

Angelou, Maya, *The Collected Autobiographies of Maya Angelou* (Random House Inc., 2004)

Aron, Elaine N., *The Highly Sensitive Person: How to Survive and Thrive When the World Overwhelms You* (Thorsons, 2017)

Beck, Martha, *Finding Your Own North Star: How to Claim the Life You Were Meant to Live* (Piatkus, 2003)

Cain, Susan, *Quiet: The Power of Introverts in a World That Can't Stop Talking* (Crown Publishing Group, 2012)

Coelho, Paulo, *The Alchemist: A Fable About Following Your Dream* (HarperCollins, 1995)

Demartini, John F., *The Breakthrough Experience: A Revolutionary New Approach to Personal Transformation* (Hay House, 2002)

Jeffers, Susan, *Feel the Fear and Do It Anyway: How to Turn Your Fear and Indecision into Confidence and Action* (Vermilion, 2007)

Johnson, Dr. Spencer, *Who Moved My Cheese: An Amazing Way to Deal with Change in Your Work and in Your Life* (Vermilion, 1999)

MY FAVORITE EVENTS AND RETREATS

Wild Voice Extravaganza with Edwin Coppard, www.realpeoplemusic.com

Seven-day juice detox with Detox International, www.detox-international.com

The Courage to Change with Malcolm Stern, www.cortijo-romero.co.uk

ABOUT THE AUTHOR

Greta Solomon is a British journalist turned writing coach and author. In 2006, she discovered a talent for helping people overcome the blocks, fears, and shame that stop them from fully expressing themselves. Through talks, workshops, and online programs, Greta teaches real-world writing techniques and inspires others to live rich, creative lives. She lives in London.